HILLSIDE LETTERS A TO Z
A Guide to Hometown Landmarks

EVELYN CORNING

Best Wishes

Evelyn Lyman Corning

Mountain Press Publishing Company
Missoula, Montana
2007

FRONT COVER:
M in Missoula, Montana; photo by Todd Goodrich, University of Montana

BACK COVER:
G in Gap, Arizona; photo by Jim Corning
R in Rexburg, Idaho; photo by Michael Lewis, Brigham Young University–Idaho
U in Uintah, Utah; Uintah City Historical Files photo

Library of Congress Cataloging-in-Publication Data

Corning, Evelyn, 1952–
    Hillside letters A to Z : a guide to hometown landmarks / Evelyn Corning.
        p. cm.
    Includes bibliographical references and index.
    ISBN 978-0-87842-533-4 (alk. paper)
    1. Historic sites—United States—Guidebooks. 2. English language—Alphabet—
Miscellanea. 3. Mimetic architecture—United States—Guidebooks. 4. Mountains—
United States—Guidebooks. 5. United States—Guidebooks. 6. United States—History,
Local. I. Title.
E159.C79 2007
973.9—dc22

                                2007000516

Printed in Hong Kong by Mantec Production Company

Mountain Press Publishing Company
P.O. Box 2399
Missoula, Montana 59806

DEDICATION

Jim, Katie, Sarah, Patrick, Amy, and Bryce
There is no hillside emblem, no matter how gigantic, that
compares with the love and support I have received from you.

CONTENTS

In 1986 my family and I were traveling through Tucson, Arizona, when we passed by the giant letter A built on a prominent hillside near the center of town. Three-year-old Patrick, who was learning his alphabet at the time, became so excited to see not only a letter that he recognized, but one that covered the entire top of a mountain, that he could hardly contain himself. Born and raised in Nebraska he had never seen anything like this before. I casually told Patrick, "Oh, that's A Mountain."

We continued traveling, and I realized that Patrick was very quiet, especially considering that he was surrounded by his three sisters, whom he was always teasing. I turned to find Patrick still staring out the window of our old Suburban. "What are you looking for, Patrick?" I asked. He turned from the window and replied, "I'm looking for B Mountain, Mom." I started to laugh, then realized he was serious. In the mind of a three-year-old learning his ABCs, if there was an A Mountain, there certainly would be a B Mountain. Our inquisitive Patrick spent the rest of the family vacation looking for B Mountain. In fact, we all did.

This experience got me wondering: Just who made A Mountain, and why? What started this phenomenon of letters on hillsides? How many giant letters are there, and where are they located? I had grown up in the West and knew there were letters scattered on mountains throughout many western states. I knew there must be a B Mountain somewhere; I just didn't know where to look. To help Patrick feel better, I promised that someday I would write him an alphabet book about the story of mountain letters . . . and now, years later, I have.

ACKNOWLEDGMENTS

This book would not exist had it not been for the help of many who contributed their expertise, their time, and their talents. An abundance of appreciation is extended to the late Dr. James J. Parsons, a professor of geography for nearly forty years at the University of California–Berkeley. His interest in hillside letters and his 1988 article in *Landscape* magazine provided the foundation for my research. Dr. Parsons was a geographer's geographer, and his contributions to the field of geography continue to grow even after his passing.

Dr. Paul F. Starrs, a renowned professor and geographer at the University of Nevada–Reno, and a former student of Dr. Parsons, has continued his mentor's interest in hillside letters. Dr. Starrs' help was invaluable; he generously gave of his expertise and time to answer my many questions. Without his knowledgeable guidance, his encouraging words, and the use of his photo collection, much of the information in this book might have remained unknown to me.

Countless others helped uncover the histories and cultural traditions associated with many of our country's hillside letters. My special thanks go to those many university and community librarians and archivists who searched old newspapers, yearbooks, and other documents for information about their local mountain monograms. These include: Shan Watkins at Colorado State University Libraries in Fort Collins; Christine Marin at Arizona State University Libraries in Tempe; William B. Boehm at New Mexico State University Library in Las Cruces; Erica Nordmeier at University of California–Berkeley's Bancroft Library; Bonnie Percival at Val A. Browning Library of Dixie State College of Utah in St. George; Robin Stanger and Karen Kearns at the Eli M. Oboler Library of Idaho State University in Pocatello; Susan Behring at the Brigham City Carnegie Library in Brigham City, Utah; Robert Sorgenfrei at Arthur Lakes Library of the Colorado School of Mines in Golden; Betsy Harper Garlish at Montana Tech Library in Butte; Barbara Van Cleave at the University of Montana–Western's Carson Library and Swysgood Technology Center; Joan Shedivy at the Skeen Library of New Mexico Tech in Socorro;

Teresa Hamann at the Mansfield Library of the University of Montana–Missoula; Donna Neal at the Deveraux Library of the South Dakota School of Mines and Technology in Rapid City; Kathryn M. Totton and Jim Bantin at the University of Nevada–Reno Library; Anne Hiller Clark at the Oregon Institute of Technology Libraries in Klamath Falls; Heather Briston at the University of Oregon's Knight Library in Eugene; Ken Kenyon at the Robert E. Kennedy Library of Cal Poly–San Luis Obispo; Ann O'Donnell at the Armacost Library of the University of Redlands in Redlands, California; Chris Bendlin and Tracey Kinnaman of Hot Springs County Library in Thermopolis, Wyoming; Gaylan Corbin at Sul Ross State University Library in Alpine, Texas; Lorraine Crouse at the University of Utah's Mariott Library in Salt Lake City; and Nancy Gauss and Patrick Muckleroy at the Leslie J. Savage Library of Western State College of Colorado in Gunnison.

Numerous school officials provided information on the history of individual letters. I deeply appreciate the help of Sara Matthews at Basic High School in Henderson, Nevada; Don Perkins at Bountiful High School in Bountiful, Utah; Susan Shurtz and Derlynne Brooks at Escalante High School in Escalante, Utah; Hal Reeder and Larry Douglass at the Intermountain Inter-tribal Indian School in Brigham City, Utah; Rae Cille Dawson at Jefferson High School in Boulder, Montana; Joe Stewart at Kelso High School in Kelso, Washington; Doug Potter at La Grande High School in La Grande, Oregon; Penny Wakida and Jean Miyahira at Lahainaluna High School in Lahaina, Hawaii; Teri McGaha at Okanogan High School in Okanogan, Washington; Ray Donnenwirth and Phil Raymond at Portola High School in Portola, California; Jay Evans at Tintic High School in Eureka, Utah; William Sorbe at Valley High School in Orderville, Utah; and Bob Nelson of Willcox High School in Willcox, Arizona.

University public relations personnel, alumni officials, and others associated with institutions of higher education were an invaluable resource for photos and current information on their schools' hillside letters. I am grateful for the help of Con Marshall at Chadron State College in Chadron, Nebraska; Natalie M. Freese at the University of California–Berkeley; Corinne Hansen at Black Hills State University in Spearfish, South Dakota; Marsha Williams at the Colorado School of Mines in Golden; Suzi Taylor at Montana State University in Bozeman; B. J. McQuirk at the University of Montana–Missoula; Mike Miller at the University of Montana–Western in Dillon; Robert Eveletho at New Mexico Tech in Socorro; Odette Richardson at Mount San Antonio College in Walnut, California; Julie Smoragiewicz and Becky Oliver of the South Dakota School of Mines and Technology; Chris Baker and Teresa Hendrix at Cal Poly in San Luis Obispo, California; Julia Cummings at the University of Redlands in Redlands, California; Dean Mortimer, former president of the Brigham Young University–Idaho Alumni Association; Paula Brewer at Snow College in Ephraim, Utah; Jim Clifton and Nancy Blanton at Sul Ross State University in Alpine, Texas; Marc Day and Elese Adams at the University of Utah in Salt Lake City; Sandy Sorwerby and Lynn Kraaima at Weber State University in Ogden, Utah; Larry Meredith at Western State College of Colorado in Gunnison; and Janet Rex at Brigham Young University in Provo, Utah.

Museum staff and city officials provided additional sources of information. I'd like to extend a special thanks to Reenie (Maureen) Ochoa of the City of Tucson, Arizona; Suzanne Turgeon of the Clark County Museum in Henderson, Nevada; Heather Trujillo of the City of Carlin, Nevada; Claudia Heller of the Duarte Historical Museum and Ed Cox of the City of Duarte, California; Chris Reed at the Pinal County Historical Society Museum in Florence, Arizona; Sue Bybee of the City of Uintah, Utah; Jennifer Johnston at the Maricopa County Usery Mountain Regional Park in Mesa, Arizona; and Cindy Zahn of the City of Zap, North Dakota.

Many local residents offered invaluable information on hillside letters. Many thanks to John W. Womack and Edith Palmer of Dillon, Montana; Laverne M. Williams and Linda Drake of Bisbee, Arizona; Carolee North of Garibaldi, Oregon; Jim Streibe of Boulder, Montana; Gary Webster of La Grande, Oregon; Gwen Gardner of Lone Pine, California; Larry Matthew and Dan Wilson of Oroville, California; Larry Simpson and Darice McVay of Van Horn, Texas; Dean Hurst of Ogden, Utah; and Robert Solem of Zap, North Dakota.

Without a doubt, some of the most valuable information on the history of these letters came through interviewing some of the letter builders: A. B. "Boomer" Simpkins, who was instrumental in the reconstruction of the C in Carlin, Nevada; David Stewart, who helped repaint the G in Moab, Utah; Jim Brown, one of three young men hired to build the H for Black Hills State University in Spearfish, South Dakota; Brett Jackson, who instigated the rebuilding of the K in Kanab, Utah; Roselee Wheeler, who assisted with the building of the Q in Quartzsite, Arizona; Mo Montijo, who helped build the S in Salome, Arizona; Lowell Mecham, who led the restoration effort of the T in Tropic, Utah; and Janice Denson, who advised the construction effort for the TB in Twin Bridges, Montana.

Finally my appreciation goes to the many professional and other photographers who supplied photos of the letters. Most are individually credited in the book, but a few of these people went beyond taking a photo and provided additional information about the letter. These include: Bill Cotton at Colorado State University in Fort Collins; Jackilyn Drake of Bisbee, Arizona; Chantiel Graves of Carlin, Nevada; Alan Heller of Duarte, California; Howard Hickson of Elko, Nevada; Cody Richardson of Boulder, Montana; Todd Goodrich at the University of Montana in Missoula; Wally Feldt at the University of Montana–Western in Dillon; Mike Lewis at Brigham Young University–Idaho in Rexburg; Richard Coffinberry of Thermopolis, Wyoming; Lisa Kunkel in Butte, Montana; and Mike Taylor at Mount San Antonio College in Walnut, California.

I want to thank numerous family and friends who helped me out in so many ways. Special gratitude has to go to my daughter, Sarah, who spent hours on the phone verifying letters and their locations, as well as to my very special friend, Sally Stockton, whose help and support was simply invaluable. And a loving thank you to my husband, Jim, who took photos, gave advice, fixed the computer, listened to my complaints, and was forever encouraging. Without him I would have given up a thousand times.

A huge thanks goes to my editor, Beth Parker, whom I have never met in person, but to whom I will always be indebted. She has quietly performed editing miracles behind the scene that have resulted in the once-in-a-lifetime experience of writing a book about the hidden history and culture of hillside letters. Thanks to Beth and all the talented people at Mountain Press Publishing Company for turning my pages of typed manuscript into a wonderful book.

LOCATIONS OF HILLSIDE LETTERS IN THE UNITED STATES

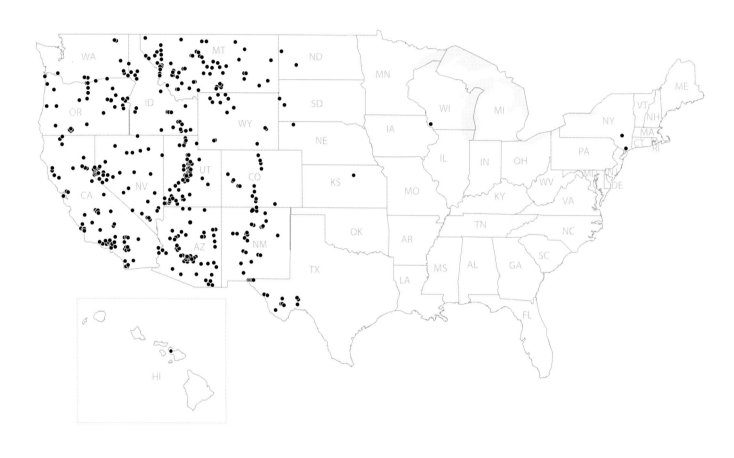

INTRODUCTION

If you live in the West you've probably seen them. Maybe you have even grown up with one overlooking your hometown or school. The first one appeared in March 1905: a sixty-foot-tall concrete C on Charter Hill overlooking the San Francisco Bay. Today this letter is nearly obscured by a grove of eucalyptus and Monterey pine trees, but the students at the University of California in Berkeley still refer to it as "the Big C." The University of Utah's U appeared less than a month later, and a Y for Brigham Young University followed a year after that. Soon there were hillside letters popping up all over the West. Little did the students of Berkeley realize that their hillside letter would launch a tradition that would change the American landscape.

A Landscape of Letters

Letters on hillsides are located all over the nation, from the University of California's C on the West Coast to Columbia University's C on the East Coast; thus we are truly a nation of hillside letters "from C to shining C." A few letters are found in countries outside the United States, but hillside letters are primarily a phenomenon of the American West, where there are vast landscapes of treeless hillsides visible for miles.

The first rash of hillside letters occurred during the early decades of the twentieth century with the establishment of public universities and land-grant colleges in the West, many of which were agricultural or mining schools—hence the abundance of hillside letters A (for "Aggies") and M (for "Miners"). The tradition was most popular before the rise of environmentalism and the growing aesthetic preference for untouched natural landscapes, but letter-building on mountain slopes has stayed alive despite controversy.

1

An exact count of hillside letters is not possible, as the number fluctuates with the creation of new letters and the disappearance of others due to neglect, destruction, or dismantling for environmental or liability reasons. Of over 400 letters throughout the United States, all but a handful are located in fourteen western states: California, Oregon, Washington, Idaho, Montana, Wyoming, Utah, Nevada, Arizona, New Mexico, North Dakota, South Dakota, Nebraska, and Texas (see map on page xii).

Why Mark a Mountain?

There is a long-held myth, perpetuated even today by some historians, that letters were placed on hillsides as landmarks for early pilots who air-dropped the mail. This is incorrect, with the exception of one hillside emblem—the word PHOENIX in Mesa, Arizona—that was built to be an air marker. The rest were constructed as community and school emblems. However, because of the proximity of some letters to airports, a few have since been designated as visual landmarks by the Federal Aviation Administration.

The first letters were proudly designed and built by students and teachers as emblems of their university or college. Later, high schools and communities large and small followed suit. Some letters commemorated the building of a long-awaited school or celebrated a team's winning streak. Even elementary schools and groups like the Boy Scouts erected letters in communities too small to have a high school. Some letters first built for schools became community emblems as the years passed. This is especially true for smaller communities.

A few hillside letters were built to honor the memory of a teacher or community member. Some letters are even more personal in significance: The eighty-foot-tall G in Glenwood, Utah, was constructed by the descendants of Archibald T. Oldroyd, the founder of Glenwood, as part of their 2003 family reunion. Gerry Chestnut, a young soldier who died in the Vietnam War, had always told his family that he knew he was really home when he saw the E above Escalante, Utah. At least one university has given permission for the ashes of a deceased alumnus to be scattered over his alma mater hillside emblem. Such strong emotional attachments to hometown letters are common. They seem to capture and elicit fond recollections of school days or sweet memories of home. These giant emblems are symbols of local identity, silently announcing to all: this is my home, my school; this is the place I love.

Paul Starrs, professor of geography at the University of Nevada–Reno, places the phenomenon of hillside letters within the broader American tradition of landscape symbols, which also include words blazoned on water towers in

The students of Meeteetse High School in Meeteetse, Wyoming, added longhorns to their hillside emblem, a fitting tribute to their school mascot, the Longhorns. —COURTESY OF MEETEETSE HIGH SCHOOL

the Midwest, and town slogans on highway "welcome to" signs across the country. Landscape symbols are messages with which local residents establish their distinctive community identity and their place on the land. What sets hillside letters apart from other landscape symbols, however, is the collective commitment, enthusiasm, and grassroots support that gets a letter built and keeps it maintained, in some cases for generations.

The ABCs of Letter-Building

Letter-builders were typically full of youthful energy and idealism, which is why so many letters are associated with schools. Students displayed uncommon leadership to inspire sometimes hundreds of people not only to believe in their ideas but also to contribute the physical effort it required to make the dream a reality. They sometimes overcame difficult obstacles, such as calculating the descriptive geometry in designing a huge letter to appear undistorted as it covered the natural contours of the mountainside, or physically moving hundreds of tons of concrete and rock without the aid of machinery.

Over the years resourceful students and local residents have come up with a variety of ways to turn a hillside into a giant monogram. Three basic types of letters have emerged: built-up letters, painted letters, and cutout letters.

Built-up Letters

Most letters are built up from the ground, typically with rocks or concrete. Though less common, other materials have been used as well, such as wood, pipes, old car tires, or metal that is cut out or shaped into the letter.

Building a letter from rock is usually very labor intensive. Students at the University of Arizona, for instance, spent Saturday after Saturday for nearly two years building their gigantic A. They cleared the site of vegetation and dug trenches to outline the letter. Then they quarried rocks and carried them to the site, and mixed the rocks with mortar and water that was carried by six-horse teams up the mountainside. Then hundreds of students filled in the letter's outline, pouring this mixture by hand. In contrast, the University of California–Berkeley's Big C, a built-up letter made entirely of concrete, was constructed by students in only two days.

Built-up letters typically get covered with whitewash or white paint after they are completed. Originally most letter-builders used whitewash (a mixture of water and lime), which was cheap to make—an important consideration with very large letters. However, the lime in whitewash can cause a chemical burn to the skin. In recent years, more and more letters are being covered in paint. Even though it is more expensive, it is safer, lasts longer, and can be more colorful. The distinction between paint and whitewash is not always made by historical sources, however, so in this book paint refers to either.

Author in front of the University of Arizona's A, an example of a letter built up with rocks, in Tucson, Arizona. —PHOTO BY JIM CORNING

Western State College students in Gunnison, Colorado, pass up buckets of whitewash to paint their W, the largest built-up hillside letter in the country (photo c. 1950).
—COURTESY OF WESTERN STATE COLLEGE OF COLORADO

Many letters are painted with a combined effort of hundreds of students, and some by just a few devoted hands. The painting of school letters is often a class activity that is part of an annual tradition during homecoming, the start of fall classes, or graduation. Painting can take anywhere from hours to weeks, depending on the labor resources. In 1982, after environmental concerns about erosion led the Forest Service to prohibit the student-led annual whitewashing of Brigham Young University's concrete Y, the school hired a helicopter to haul paint, sprayers, and water. Four men with 155 gallons of paint had the job completed in twelve hours.

A student of Dixie State College in St. George, Utah, helps paint the rock D during the college's annual D Week celebration (photo c. 1980). —COURTESY OF VAL A. BROWNING LIBRARY, DIXIE STATE COLLEGE OF UTAH

The most common paint color is white, but school colors are also common. Some built-up letters get coats of red, white, and blue to display their community's patriotism. Others get painted green for St. Patrick's Day, or black as a form of protest.

By late afternoon of September 11, 2001, students at Arizona State University in Tempe had painted their A with red, white, and blue stars and stripes to show their support for a grieving nation. —ARIZONA STATE UNIVERSITY PHOTO

Painted Letters

Some letters are formed simply by being painted on the mountainside. This is often the case where the hillside is fairly smooth and flat with little or no vegetation, and especially on a slope too steep for a built-up letter, such as on the rock face of a cliff. Unlike the construction of most built-up letters, which may require the effort of many people, only a few hands are needed for painted letters.

Painted letters can be difficult to maintain. Letters painted low in the foothills, such as the P for Page, Arizona, are sometimes the target of vandals and rivals. But letters painted in areas not easily accessed by vandals are also less accessible to those who maintain them. Maintenance of Grand County

This G is painted high on a rock face above the small Navajo community of Gap, Arizona. —PHOTO BY JIM CORNING

Letters painted low in the foothills, such as the P for Page, Arizona, are sometimes the target of vandals and rivals. —PHOTO BY JAMES J. PARSONS; COURTESY OF PAUL F. STARRS, UNIVERSITY OF NEVADA–RENO

High School's Big G in Moab, Utah, requires painters to strap on harnesses and rappel off the high red sandstone cliff that provides the natural canvas for this painted letter (see photo on page 17).

Cutout Letters

The least common type of letter construction is the cutout letter, formed by removing vegetation to create the shape of a letter. Occasionally cutout letters have been formed by pouring lime on a grassy hillside. Cutout letters are best seen when they are lighted or when the snow falls and fills in the cleared area, making the letter stand out against the wooded hillside.

Cutout letters have two major problems. First, they require more frequent maintenance to keep the vegetation from obscuring the letter. Second,

This cutout A in Alton, Utah, is most visible when lightly dusted with snow. —PHOTO BY TYSON JUDD

removing vegetation from a hillside can create erosion problems. These two reasons might account for the fact that cutout letters are rare, comprising less than 2 percent of all hillside letters.

Illuminating Letters

The practice of lighting letters at night for homecoming or other special occasions, such as prom, graduation, or a victorious game, is a long-held tradition associated with many of these giant monograms. Some emblems are illuminated by electric lights powered by solar panels or generators. The lights for the M at the Colorado School of Mines are entirely computer automated and remote controlled, thanks to the school's engineering students.

Other schools have used flares, oil, gasoline, and even cans filled with corncobs to light their letter. Through the years, the students of Brigham Young University employed a number of ingenious methods to light up their hundred-plus-year-old Y, such as outlining the letter with bales of cotton dipped in tar and pitch, or torching "goop balls" made from a variety of materials, from old dormitory mattress stuffing soaked in motor oil to a mixture of grease and feathers. Students of Weber State University in Ogden, Utah, set the entire mountainside on fire when igniting their kerosene-soaked letter on Homecoming Day in 1957.

Perhaps the most dramatic lighting of a hillside letter is Arizona State University's Lantern Walk, led by the president of the university. Each year students retrace the steps of thousands of students before them who carried a lighted candle or lantern up Tempe Butte. The tradition began in 1917, a year before the school built its first hillside letter on the butte. Today hundreds of students, alumni, and supporters of the university participate in this event, which occurs the night before the homecoming football game and culminates in the lighting of the A over Sun Devil Stadium.

The Miners' M in Golden, Colorado, has been lighted continuously since 1931.
—PHOTO BY TOM COOPER; COURTESY OF THE COLORADO SCHOOL OF MINES

Customs, Conflicts, and Controversies

Many hillside letters are the focus of traditions, rituals, and special events. Besides the painting and lighting of letters, activities include pilgrimages up the hill, picnics on the hillside, sliding down mud or wet paint, hillside rivalries, and late-night raids.

In some cases, the natural affection of students for their school's giant emblem is forged into fierce allegiance through an initiation ritual. Typically, older students direct newer students in the performance of a task related to maintenance of the letter. At the Colorado School of Mines, for example, when incoming freshmen whitewash their M, they bring with them a rock to add to the letter, which they retrieve when they graduate. In some cases, tradition

The University of Oregon's O in Eugene was one of the oldest letters in the country before it met its demise in the intense rivalry between the University of Oregon and Oregon State University.
—IMAGE COURTESY OF SPECIAL COLLECTIONS AND UNIVERSITY ARCHIVES, UNIVERSITY OF OREGON LIBRARIES

dictates that a task be performed in ridiculous or humiliating attire. Years ago, freshmen in Highwood, Montana, had to whitewash their H while dressed in diapers and construction boots. The freshmen at Boron High School in Boron, California, used to carry the seniors to the top of B Hill before painting their rock B with toothbrushes. Much like the freshmen in Boron, the freshmen of Mount San Antonio College in Walnut, California, were once required to clean their school's two massive monograms using toothbrushes while the sophomores supervised.

Hillside letters, as symbols of identity and pride, sometimes become battlegrounds for rival groups. This is especially true if rival schools are in close proximity to each other. A good example is the University of Oregon's fifty-foot O, first made from rocks on Skinner Butte by the junior class in 1908. The O was stolen so many times over the years by the students of Oregon State University in Corvallis, just north of Eugene, that in the early 1950s it was reconstructed of concrete and wood. Unable to remove it, the students of Oregon State dynamited it in 1952, and again in 1953. By 1957, the students at the University of Oregon felt the Oregon State students had "contaminated" their emblem to such an extent that they burned their own letter, and the following year they built a metal O embedded in concrete. Soon afterwards the Oregon State students cut the O into sections and took it to their campus in Corvallis. After several months it was returned, reassembled, and reinstalled, only to be stolen again. The last time anyone at the University of Oregon can remember seeing their O was in 1972.

A more common expression of rivalry occurs when students paint a rival school's letter their own school colors, most often late at night. This is a longstanding pregame tradition at many schools, and some have even instituted the use of student guards. Brigham Young University has plastic-wrapped the school's Y to prevent nighttime attacks by their rivals before sporting events. Berkeley's century-old Big C has for decades been guarded by students when they play their archrival, Stanford. In 1961, a group of Stanford engineering students, using jackhammers and a helicopter, landed on Charter Hill and in broad daylight turned the Big C into a red S.

Cases of letter altering sometimes have nothing to do with rivalry. At one time, students of Loyola Sacred Heart High School in Missoula, Montana, frequently woke to find that their rock L on Mount Jumbo was transformed overnight by anonymous individuals using Mount Jumbo as a message board. When Mount Jumbo became city-owned open space in the 1990s, it sparked a flurry of messages on the mountain. Every morning for days, the whitewashed rocks of the L would appear in new forms, from marriage proposals and memorials to political statements. The students of Loyola, responsible for

The whitewashed rocks of Loyola Sacred Heart's L on Mount Jumbo in Missoula, Montana, were frequently reshaped into other symbols and messages before the letter was filled with concrete in 2001. Now any messages must include the giant L. —PHOTO BY TOM BAUER

maintaining the L since it was built in 1961, would trudge up the mountain and spend hours replacing the white rocks in their L-shaped frame, until finally, with the help of parents, alumni, and a hired helicopter, they filled the L with concrete in 2001. That has reduced activity around the letter, but does not prevent occasional hillside bulletins.

Although the creation of most hillside letters emerged amid widespread local support, they were not always wanted by everyone. Many people see letters on hills as graffiti. Because of this, a number of letters have been removed. Even the building of the Big C in Berkeley over a hundred years ago brought a storm of community and faculty protests when it was announced. The sudden disappearance of the seventy-six-year-old Big G in Moab, Utah, was carried out under a cloak of secrecy, presumably by environmentally motivated newcomers to the community. Ansel Adams, the great photographer of the early twentieth century, brushed out Lone Pine's LP in his famous photo of California's Alabama Hills. One of the more recent hillside letters built in a metropolitan area, Eldorado High School's E in Las Vegas, Nevada, took three

Grand County High School alumni Guy Johnston and Davy Stewart rappelled off a cliff in Moab, Utah, to restore the Big G after its mysterious disappearance. —PHOTO BY TONI JOHNSTON

years, a lawyer, and a whole lot of paperwork before the students (officially) applied a single drop of whitewash in 1978.

Despite environmental and aesthetic controversy, most hillside letters are cherished emblems of a school or community. Whether hillside letters are community symbols or graffiti, they are a fascinating part of our Western culture, and their history deserves to be recorded. The late James J. Parsons, professor of geography at the University of California–Berkeley and researcher of hillside letters, wrote, "The letter on the mountain is a subject without a literature. However, for travelers in the arid West the letters are anchors to the eye, adding diversity and interest to the natural beauty of the landscape." So enjoy the journey as you discover some of the stories of America's hillside letters from A to Z.

A AGGIES OF COLORADO STATE UNIVERSITY
Fort Collins, Colorado

For some time, the students of the Agricultural College of Colorado (now Colorado State University) in Fort Collins, Colorado, had been trying to get the cooperation of the entire student body to build an A as their school landmark. At a special assembly in December 1923, Natt Dodge, the student body president, led the charge that finally got the students, or "Aggies," their A.

The hill they chose was the Hog-Back, west of the college. Three engineering students, Don Jones, Charles Ross, and Dick Barton, laid out the A's outline on the hill, surveying and staking out the boundaries of the letter. Carl Carpenter was one of the students assigned to mine rocks higher up on the mountainside; these would be used to fill in the letter's outline. Carpenter recalled later that they used about a hundred pounds of picric acid (a high explosive) to blast out the hillside, and it was a miracle no one got hurt by rolling and flying rocks—the men were using the explosives at the same time other students below were carrying rocks to place within the A's outline.

While male students supplied the muscle, the school's military department supplied vehicles for transporting materials, and female students helped by feeding all the hungry laborers. The giant A was completed in less than six hours. However, when viewed from campus the A appeared too short. The following year the student body returned to the Hog-Back and extended the legs of the A about a hundred feet down, and they lowered the crossbar to give

The A on the Hog-Back is the hillside letter of the Aggies of Colorado State University in Fort Collins.
—COLORADO STATE UNIVERSITY PHOTO

the letter a more balanced look. Today it is 450 feet from top to bottom. The freshman football players of Colorado State University and members of the Sigma Alpha Epsilon fraternity are responsible for maintaining the Aggies' A.

A AGGIES OF NEW MEXICO STATE UNIVERSITY
Las Cruces, New Mexico

On April Fools' Day in 1920, the New Mexico College of Agriculture and Mechanic Arts students—called the "Aggies"—painted their new built-up letter A on the hillside overlooking their campus in Las Cruces, New Mexico. The entire student body had the day off because of the tremendous task of hand-carrying the whitewash a half-mile up the steep slope of Tortugas Mountain at the eastern edge of the college campus. As was the case at other

19

The A for the Aggies of New Mexico State University is a prominent landmark that overlooks the campus and community of Las Cruces, New Mexico. —PHOTO BY JIM CORNING

universities and colleges during this time, the men provided the labor and the women provided lunch.

The following year, the students decided that if their whitewashed A was to be a permanent fixture, it must be more accurately surveyed. Two days prior to the 1921 scheduled whitewashing of the letter, a small group of students surveyed a new site, situating the emblem so that it would be more aesthetically pleasing when viewed from the campus. They patterned this A after the monogram worn by the football lettermen.

On the day of the whitewashing, students spent the entire morning carrying the rocks from the first A and placing them within the laid-out boundaries of the new A. Afterwards the men's efforts were rewarded not only with lunch supplied by the women, but with the unexpected bonus of bananas, lemonade, and ice cream provided by Professor Goddard and Robert W. Clothier, president of the college.

In 1960, the New Mexico College of Agriculture and Mechanic Arts changed its name to New Mexico State University. For many years it was the job of the freshman class to paint the A with the assistance of the seniors. Currently the university's Greek organizations maintain the seventy-five-plus-year-old letter each spring as part of their Aggie Day, or A Day, festivities.

A ARIZONA STATE UNIVERSITY
Tempe, Arizona

In 1917 the senior and freshman classes of Tempe Normal School of Arizona began a tradition of hiking at night to the top of Tempe Butte, a rocky volcanic butte at the edge of the main campus. The seniors held lanterns to light the way for the freshmen as they trudged to the top of the hill. Upon their arrival, the senior class president delivered a speech, and the lanterns, representing the standards and ideals of the school, were then passed from the seniors to the freshmen. This became known as the Lantern Walk.

A year later, the senior class of 1918 built the school's first letter on Tempe Butte near where the Lantern Walk culminated. It was a petite 36-by-36-foot letter N constructed out of boulders to represent Tempe Normal School of Arizona. Then in 1923, the N was reconstructed and enlarged. Two years later the school changed its name to Tempe State Teachers College, and the N was made into a T, retaining one leg of the old N. In 1928 the school changed its name again, this time to Arizona State Teachers College.

This name change did not affect the school's hillside letter until 1938, when the letter A replaced the old T on Tempe Butte. This A watched over the

Arizona State University's A has been on Tempe Butte since 1928. —PHOTO BY KATIE CORNING

campus until 1952, when a bomb blast nearly demolished the letter. The *Arizona Republic*, a local newspaper, reported that the blast was a prank, and it was assumed that students from nearby rival University of Arizona were responsible. The present A was rebuilt in 1955; it is sixty feet long and constructed of reinforced steel and concrete.

The Student Alumni Association has been overseeing the A's maintenance since the 1980s. This A is painted more frequently than any other hillside letter. (See photo on page 8.) In 2005 alone, the A was painted sixty-five times, requiring 130 coats, or 1,300 gallons, of paint. Since the letter was built, all the additional paint has added about 4 inches to the letter's original thickness of 16 inches.

Every year student guards protect the A against attacks by the University of Arizona Wildcats the week before their annual football game. The Lantern

Students of Arizona State University paint their letter A gold on the hillside overlooking Tempe.
—ARIZONA STATE UNIVERSITY PHOTO

Walk up Tempe Butte still occurs the night before homecoming, but now it is led by the president of Arizona State University and is the means by which the Sun Devils annually light their golden A.

A UNIVERSITY OF ARIZONA
Tucson, Arizona

A Mountain, as the locals call it, is a prominent ridge along the Tucson Mountains west of Tucson, Arizona, in the beautiful Sonoran Desert. The giant A on the slope, overlooking downtown Tucson and the Tucson Convention Center, stands for the University of Arizona.

The A in Tucson, Arizona, is maintained by the city. It was painted patriotic colors in 2003.
—PHOTO BY CURT FINSTER

In 1885 Arizona's territorial legislature gave the community of Tucson $25,000 to develop a new university, but they could find no one willing to donate the land. The city had decided to return the money when two generous gamblers and a saloonkeeper stepped forward to donate forty acres of land. The university opened its doors in 1891 with thirty-two students and six teachers.

Eight years later, the school's first football team formed; they were a rather mediocre squad, however. As a result, in 1914 the students of the University of Arizona launched a petition requesting that the administration hire the local Tucson High School coach, J. F. "Pops" McKale. McKale's high school teams were unbeatable—they even beat the university team. The university president, A. H. Wilde, who was not much of a football fan, reluctantly agreed. They hired McKale, and the football team played their first game of the season against Occidental College in Los Angeles, one of California's gridiron powerhouses of the time. Occidental won 14-0. However, because the Arizona team had shown such spirit and fight, a *Los Angeles Times* reporter nicknamed them "the Wildcats." The name stuck, and the team and its mascot became the Arizona Wildcats.

The University of Arizona played its second game of the 1914 season against Pomona College on Thanksgiving Day, and to everyone's surprise, the visiting Wildcats won a sensational 7-6 victory on Pomona's field. Two years earlier, Pomona College had built a P on their hillside. After Arizona's great win, one of the star football players, Albert Condon, suggested to his civil engineering class that the University of Arizona build a letter of its own.

The work began in 1914, and it took nearly two years to complete the rock-and-mortar letter A under the direction of Condon, who became the school's student body president in 1915. The site was first cleared of cactus and shrubbery; next the students dug wide trenches by hand for the foundation of the entire letter. They built the letter using the black basalt rock quarried from the hillside, and then cemented the rocks together using mortar and water hauled in by six-horse teams. Some of the remaining rocks were used to build early homes at the base of the mountain, as well as the "Rock Wall" that still surrounds part of the university campus historic district.

The University of Arizona's A is 70 feet wide, 160 feet long, and about 5 feet thick from the base of the underground foundation to the letter's top surface (see photo on page 5). It was the first of approximately fifty hillside letters built in Arizona. The location chosen for this emblem was Sentinel Peak, a place of great importance to the native people of Tucson, who called the peak Stookzone, meaning "water at the foot of black mountain." It is from this peak that Tucson got its name. Now Sentinel Peak is known as "A Mountain."

In the beginning, University of Arizona students maintained, painted, and lighted the A, but currently this local landmark is cared for by the city of Tucson. It is no longer lighted, but it is painted professionally for maintenance once a year, and sometimes more frequently—such as when rival Arizona State University students from Tempe, armed with paintbrushes, attack the A, changing it from red, white, and blue, to red, yellow, and blue. Many times on St. Patrick's Day, celebrants have given the monogram a fresh coat of green paint during the night. Today, A Mountain is a favorite place for many Tucsonans to celebrate the Fourth of July and to watch the fireworks illuminate the giant A first built to celebrate the victorious Wildcat football team of 1914.

University of Arizona students building the A in 1916.
—SPECIAL COLLECTIONS, UNIVERSITY OF ARIZONA LIBRARY

	NAME	LOCATION	NOTE
A	Adrian High School	Adrian, OR	The A was built in the 1940s.
A	Aggies of Colorado State University	Fort Collins, CO	Featured on page18.
A	Aggies of New Mexico State University	Las Cruces, NM	Featured on page 19.
A	Aggies of Utah State University	Logan, UT	In 1947 the A was built in cutout style because the dean of students thought letters on hills were "tacky" and would only approve a less visible, less permanent cutout letter. It was lighted annually for homecoming by the Sigma Chi fraternity using two-hundred-gallon cans filled with diesel fuel and gunny-sacks. It was last lighted in 1993. Houses now fill the land formerly occupied by the A.
A	Ajo	Ajo, AZ	Rock letter built in 1939; represents both Ajo High School and the community.
A	Alamogordo High School	Alamogordo, NM	No longer maintained by the high school students; but the high school alumni repainted it in 2006.
A	Alexander	Alexander, ND	Represents both Alexander High School and the community; maintained by the community.
A	Alpine High School	Alpine, TX	Rock letter maintained annually by the seniors and lighted for homecoming.
A	Alton	Alton, UT	One of only a few cutout letters, it was designed in 1952 by a local youth who felt that his community, which was too small to have a school, should at least have a hillside letter. It is maintained by the community. See photo on page 11.
A	Amity	Amity, OR	The A stood for the community and school but was removed.
A	Anaconda High School	Anaconda, MT	Built in 1918; cared for by senior class members and their parents.
A	Arco High School	Arco, ID	The school is now closed and the letter is no longer maintained, but the A and many numbers representing class years are still visible.On a hillside the locals call Number Hill is a rock A that originally stood for the old Arco High School, which closed in 1949. Since 1920 the students of Arco have painted their class year near the old rock A. The hill now has over eighty graduation years and has become somewhat of a tourist attraction; it can be seen from U.S. 93.

	NAME	LOCATION	NOTE
A	Arizona State University	Tempe, AZ	Featured on page 21. See also photo on page 8.
A	Arlee	Arlee, MT	Represents Arlee High School and the community; lighted annually during the homecoming football game.
A	Arlington	Arlington, OR	Represents both Arlington High School and the community; cared for by the senior class.
A	Ash Fork	Ash Fork, AZ	The rock A was first built and maintained by students of Ash Fork High School, but recently it has been cared for by community groups.
A	Asotin-Anatone High School	Asotin, WA	Rock letter maintained annually by the students.
A	Austin	Austin, NV	Represents Austin High School and the community; painted annually by the freshmen.
A	Austin High School	El Paso, TX	Refurbished and lighted in 2003 after some years of neglect.
A	Azusa	Azusa, CA	Each fall starting in 1958, the football team of Azusa High School announced the upcoming football season by forming a large A with chalk on a nearby hillside. Rain would wash away the chalk A by the following year. This annual tradition continued until 1991, when the school board banned the practice following a car accident involving students on their way to the A. In 2005, after nearly a year of planning, a community group called the "A Team" constructed a permanent A using white river rocks, nylon tarps, and rebar. This 10-foot-wide an 80-foot-long A can be seen from Interstate 210.
A	University of Arizona	Tucson, AZ	Featured on page 23. See also photo on page 5.

B BASIC HIGH SCHOOL
Henderson, Nevada

The giant B located in the volcanic foothills of the River Range near Henderson, Nevada, stands for Basic High School. Henderson, now one of the fastest growing communities in the nation, was once in such decline that it was almost sold as war surplus property by the U.S. government.

During World War II, the Basic Magnesium industrial plant on the outskirts of Las Vegas supplied the U.S. War Department with much-needed magnesium for ammunition and airplane parts. Government housing, much of which consisted of plywood sheets screwed together and placed upon railroad ties, was built near the plant for workers. During the war there were as many as 14,000 employees working at the plant and living in and around the Basic Townsite, but when the war ended and demand for magnesium diminished, most of these employees moved away, leaving homes vacant, closing the only high school, and devastating the local economy. In 1947 the U.S. War Assets Administration deemed the townsite war surplus, describing it in a sales brochure as "a complete community establishment, providing housing and recreation for approximately 3,500 persons." Had it not been for the Nevada state legislature's purchase of the plant and townsite, this community might have become just one more ghost town in the West.

In 1953 the town had grown so much that Henderson incorporated and Basic High School reopened in a new location. The students of Basic High built a B

29

Henderson, Nevada, once had two Bs, but now only this one remains. It is located in the foothills east of town and stands for Basic High School.

—PHOTO BY SARA MATHEWS

out of rocks high on the east side of Black Mountain. This B was whitewashed and lighted with cans of oil and bonfires until 1972, when the school constructed another B in the foothills on the east side of town, to coincide with the opening of a new Basic High School. The old Basic B was then given to the students of Burkholder Junior High, which took over the old school building when Basic High moved out. Now Henderson had two hometown landmarks, both of which were Bs.

As Henderson continued to grow, Foothill High School was built, giving Basic High School their first hometown rival. Sometime later, the old Burkholder school building was closed, and Foothill High School took over the old letter B on Black Mountain. However, every time the students of Foothill High reshaped the B into an F, it would somehow change back into a B. After a while, it was discovered that it was not the students of the new Basic High changing the letter, but the alumni of the first Basic. Try as they might, the Foothill students couldn't keep the F from changing into a B. So the school officials at Foothill High School conceded and let it return to a B.

Until 2006, Henderson had two Bs—one on the foothills for the students of the new Basic High School, and an older B on Black Mountain claimed by the alumni of the former Basic High. In that year, the old B on Black Mountain was removed to make room for more homes.

B BEAVERHEAD COUNTY HIGH SCHOOL
Dillon, Montana

Dillon, Montana, the seat of Beaverhead County, is located in a stunning setting of ranch land and mountain ranges in the southwest corner of the state. Dillon has two hillside letters: a B for Beaverhead County High School, and an M for the University of Montana–Western, formerly known as Montana State Normal College.

One night in the spring of 1930, years before Beaverhead County High School built its hillside B, a few high school students, wanting a giant emblem of their own, decided to make some changes in the college's M. The following account appeared in the local newspaper, the *Message*:

> "Look at the Big M" was heard on every corner this morning. But when you got where you could see it, it was a Big B and thereby hangs a long tale. The Beavers, true to their name had transformed a mountain in a few hours. They are reported to have started to work on the M at 7 last night and at 10 were finished, but not without a battle from the Normal boys, who on hearing what was taking place went in force to protect their letter.
>
> From all reports a battle royal took place and one Beaver, George Judge, was slightly injured on the head with a flying missile. Normalites were busy most of the morning in tearing up the B and rebuilding their M which was completed before noon.

But the *Message* didn't have the whole story. Edwin Kellner, one of the high school students involved in the prank, later wrote about this night:

The whitewashed rock B for Beaverhead County High School can be seen west of Interstate 15. —PHOTO BY WALLY FELDT

During World War II, the residents of Bisbee, Arizona, would not light their hillside emblem, fearing that it might make their small mining town a clear target for enemy bombers. —PHOTO BY JACKILYN DRAKE

When we came back down from the River Road at 10 p.m. there were some fellows from the Normal waiting for us and a little scuffling took place but nothing serious. The part I remember best was the next morning when A. T. Peterson, the principal, called an assembly and announced sternly, " . . . anyone who was involved get back up there and change the B back to an M." As you might expect the seniors didn't go back, only a small bunch of naïve guys like myself. There was no help from the Normal men.

It would be another thirty-four years before the students of Beaverhead County High School got their B. The Beavers' Letterman Club, also known as the B Club, constructed a built-up letter of rocks on a foothill west of Dillon in 1964. The high school students still paint and maintain their monogram each year and have since left the university's M alone.

B BISBEE
Bisbee, Arizona

The rock B on Chihuahua Hill, built by two young men during a driving rainstorm in 1929, has become a landmark of Bisbee, Arizona, a former mining town full of Old West charm in the southeast corner of the state. Bisbee is a community that cherishes its past and has tried hard to preserve it for others to enjoy. The town was once known as "the Queen of the Copper Camps." Today Bisbee contains a number of historic homes and museums, and it even provides a historical tour that travels deep into an old abandoned copper mine.

Over three thousand people are estimated to have been involved in the upkeep of Bisbee's B throughout the years. In the early years of maintenance, the B, which is a built-up letter constructed of rocks, was whitewashed by the Bisbee High School freshmen as part of their initiation. But when students were injured by the lime used in the whitewash, the job was turned over to other school groups, presumably more responsible than the incoming freshmen. The school has always lighted the B—first using diesel fuel and rags, then later electricity—for homecoming, except during World War II, when the townsfolk thought that enemy planes might see their lighted B and head for Bisbee.

A number of years ago the mayor of Bisbee, Laverne Williams, noticed a couple of people up on the hill near the B one evening and sent a police officer to check it out. The officer found two young men who were staying with their sweethearts at a local bed-and-breakfast. Since the view from the bed-and-breakfast was Bisbee's B, the young men decided to climb the hill and rearrange the whitewashed rocks to spell out "I Love You," hoping to impress their sweethearts with their handiwork. However, the officer wasn't about to let anyone mess with the town's emblem, even for love, and sent the two young men back down the hill. They would have to come up with another way to impress their sweethearts.

The town's commitment to history is the major reason the Bisbee Rotary Club began renovating the rock B in 2005. First the group refurbished the old electric lights. Next they restored the retaining wall that keeps the white rocks of the B from rolling down the hill. Finally, they painted the B with reflective paint, giving the old B that has watched over Bisbee for more than seven decades a total facelift.

Today you can see the B not only on the hillside overlooking Bisbee but also on the masthead of the local paper, the *Bisbee Daily Review*.

B BOUNTIFUL HIGH SCHOOL
Bountiful, Utah

The students of Bountiful High School, located in Bountiful, Utah, just north of Salt Lake City, built a small rock B along the Wasatch front on the south side of town. No one knows when it was first built, but the students kept it whitewashed until 1975. When their hometown rival, Viewmont High School, built a large concrete V a little farther north, the students, faculty, and parents of Bountiful High School decided it was time to update the old B. With donated materials, they went to work, constructing a new and much larger built-up concrete B that could be illuminated with electric lights.

The site on which the B was constructed has such a steep slope that when the students paint their letter they are required to wear a safety harness with ropes to keep them from falling. Despite the steepness, however, houses began covering the mountainside, and by the late 1970s the property under the B became very valuable. A developer wanted to buy it, but the students were determined to keep their B. They began raising money to buy the property themselves. The owner of the land was so impressed with their efforts that he changed his mind and donated the property to the school.

Today, the students of Bountiful High School light their B twice a year: once in the fall for homecoming, and again in the spring for graduation.

Bountiful High School's B has a commanding view of the city of Bountiful, Utah.
—PHOTO BY PATRICK CORNING

	NAME	LOCATION	NOTE
B	Baker High School	Baker City, OR	Built in the late 1970s and still maintained by the seniors.
B	Balmorhea	Balmorhea, TX	Visible but no longer maintained.
B	Banner	Banner, CA	The giant B is still visible, but it is uncertain who maintains it.
B	Barstow High School	Barstow, CA	First built out of rocks in 1958 by the sophomores, later it was reconstructed of concrete. It is still maintained by the students.
B	Basic High School	Henderson, NV	Featured on page 29.
BM	Battle Mountain	Battle Mountain, NV	The BM was built in 1925, and is maintained by the county.
BR	Bear River High School	Garland, UT	The letters are presently maintained by the high school key club.
B	Beatty High School	Beatty, NV	Constructed in 1971 by the students.
B	Beaver High School	Beaver, UT	One of the oldest high school letters in Utah, it was probably built between 1911 and 1920; represents both Beaver High School and the community of Beaver. Formerly the B was an M, which stood for Murdock Academy until it closed. The B is maintained by the students.
B	Beaverhead County High School	Dillon, MT	Featured on page 31.
BL	Ben Lomond High School	Ogden, UT	Maintained by the students.
B	Bernalillo High School	Bernalillo, NM	Visible along Interstate 25 but no longer cared for.
B	Bisbee	Bisbee, AZ	Featured on page 33.
B	Boise	Boise, ID	Built by the students of Boise High School during the 1960s, it is still maintained by the students but is now considered a community letter.
B	Boron High School	Boron, CA	Built in 1960 to commemorate the opening of Boron High School. In the past, the freshmen had to carry the seniors up B Hill and then paint the B with toothbrushes. The freshmen still maintain the B annually.
BC	Boulder City	Boulder City, NV	The first hillside letter in Boulder City was a B built about 1940; it was later removed and a B was painted on the water tower. In 1987 the students of Boulder City High School built a giant rock BC, which represents both the school and the community. It can be seen along U.S. 93.

	NAME	LOCATION	NOTE
B	Bountiful High School	Bountiful, UT	Featured on page 34
B	Bouse	Bouse, AZ	A rock letter maintained and whitewashed by the Boy Scouts and other community groups.
B	Bowie High School	El Paso, TX	Built in 1945; no longer maintained by the school but still visible.
B	Box Elder High School	Brigham City, UT	A built-up letter maintained by the students.
B	Bozeman High School	Bozeman, MT	Fading and no longer maintained.
B	Branson High School	Branson, CO	Built during the 1940s; it is no longer repainted but is still visible along Route 389.
B	Braves of Sanders Middle School	Sanders, AZ	Cared for by the students.
B	Bridger High School	Bridger, MT	The freshmen whitewash the B under the direction of the seniors, all supervised by adult chaperones.
B	Broadus	Broadus, MT	Fading and no longer maintained.
BV	Bryce Valley High School	Tropic, UT	See story and photo on pages 155–56.
B	Burbank	Burbank, CA	The very faded B near Glenoaks and Magnolia Boulevards in Burbank is believed to have been the emblem of Burbank High School; however, school officials are unsure. It is no longer maintained but is still visible.
B	Burlington High School	Burlington, WY	Maintained annually by the student council; visible from Route 30.
BR	Burnt River School	Unity, OR	As part of freshman initiation at this K–12 school, the seniors help the freshmen paint the rock BR. Then the seniors place their class year below the letters.
B	Burroughs High School	Ridgecrest, CA	The B is located on the grounds of the Naval Air Weapons Station, and for decades the seniors of Burroughs High School have been welcomed onto the base to paint their letter for homecoming.
B	Butte City	Butte City, ID	No longer maintained and fading from view.
B	Butte County High School	Arco, ID	Before the new Butte County High School was built, the students attended Butte High School and built a rock B. The letter is not maintained by the new school but is still visible.

C CARLIN
Carlin, Nevada

In a lush Nevada valley along the Humboldt River west of Elko, Carlin calls itself the City by the "C." This community of about 2,400 residents has always been proud of its hillside letter and through the years has gone to great lengths to preserve it. Carlin's early history is linked to mining and the railroad. When the students of Carlin High School first built the C sometime in the 1920s, they constructed it from railroad ties. This seemed a fitting tribute not only to the community, but also to the school whose team was called the Railroaders. For three quarters of a century the school and community kept the C whitewashed and maintained.

In 1999 an open range fire raged out of control along the hillside overlooking Carlin. In no time at all the old C that lay in its path caught on fire. For three long days, the community stood by and helplessly watched as the C's old creosote-soaked railroad ties slowly burned on the blackened hillside. Shortly afterwards, the townspeople gathered to discuss how they might rebuild their C with materials that would last and not catch on fire.

Boomer Simpkins, a retired railroader and a supporter of the C, got an idea. He had seen a road crew removing old metal guardrails along the highway. He thought the rails might be just what they were looking for to rebuild the C. So Boomer drove to Elko and asked the head of the highway department if the old guardrails could be used for the C in Carlin. He was told no. But that didn't

After the original C for Carlin, Nevada, was destroyed by a range fire, the community rebuilt this C out of used guardrail to ensure that it would last. —PHOTO BY CHANTIEL GRAVES

stop Boomer: he called his U.S. senator, who called the governor, and not long after that Boomer received a phone call from the highway official in Elko, who said that the old guardrails were now available.

Later that year, a group of city employees and community volunteers reconstructed 488 pieces of highway guardrail into a new C. The material chosen for Carlin's new emblem was as symbolic as the railroad ties had been in the past, because now Carlin's economy is based upon the nearby interstate highway rather than on the railroad industry.

After the metal C was constructed, volunteers painted their new monogram with thirty-five gallons of high-gloss white enamel paint. If the new hillside emblem that overlooks the City by the "C" seems to have a special glow, it is because, mixed in with the paint, six hundred pounds of reflective glass beads (the kind used to illuminate painted lines on roads) give Carlin's C a little sparkle.

C CHADRON STATE COLLEGE
Chadron, Nebraska

A mathematics instructor named T. A. F. Williams is credited with the well-designed C in the southern foothills overlooking Chadron State College in Chadron, Nebraska. No one knows what inspired Williams to build the only hillside letter in the state, but by 1924 a concrete C graced this panhandle community.

Williams first enlisted a former student by the name of Phillips to assist him in the design of the letter. Then, to make sure the measurements and distances were correct, Williams turned to the aid of his wife, who helped him string muslin along the staked outline of the C. Later, they walked to the north edge of Chadron College to see how the letter might look.

For years the concrete C has been painted white by the incoming freshmen, which often means that the young men of the class pour paint over the letter and then give the girls a ride on the C by sliding them down the steep, slippery letter. Through the years the C has been the object of pride and creativity for the students of Chadron State College. Some students have painted it various colors; others have immortalized it in verse:

> Men will come and men will pass.
> Class will follow class.
> But the C will remain in any event.
> Because it's made of Portland Cement.

The C graces the grassy hillside in Chadron, Nebraska. —PHOTO BY DANIEL BINKARD

Chadron State College's C after the Spotted Tail fire in 2006. —PHOTO BY DANIEL BINKARD

In the summer of 2006, those words became prophetic when Chadron State College was threatened by the Spotted Tail fire, a 40,000-acre wildfire burning out of control. The fire destroyed three local homes and blackened C Hill, but the concrete landmark over Chadron remained unharmed.

C COSTILLA
Costilla, New Mexico

Throughout the West there are a number of ghost towns or abandoned schools with faded hillside letters still keeping watch over these deserted sites. We have no record of when students of the Stewart Indian School, which was

The abandoned building and the crude hillside C are reminders of what was once the town of Costilla, New Mexico.
—PHOTO BY PAUL F. STARRS, UNIVERSITY OF NEVADA–RENO

open for ninety years, built a small rock S, still faintly visible, in Carson City, Nevada. Randsburg, California, calls itself "a living ghost town." Randsburg has about eighty year-round residents, who maintain a few shops for curious tourists and also spruce up the old rock R with a new coat of paint whenever it needs it. Ludlow, California, is a true ghost town, where a fading L overlooks what was once a mining town of nearly two thousand residents. Ludlow was once a bustling rest stop along America's mother highway, until Interstate 40 was built and local townspeople lost their businesses and were forced to relocate.

Another ghost town with a hillside letter is Costilla, New Mexico. Costilla was a small Spanish village that had its beginnings in the early 1880s. The word "Costilla," Spanish for "rib," refers to the riblike ridges along the mountain range that slope to the valley floor. It was along such a slope that the long-ago residents of Costilla constructed the built-up rock C. The letter was maintained first by the high school students, and then, after the high school closed, by the elementary school students. Today this lonesome C seems to speak of Costilla's better days.

C UNIVERSITY OF CALIFORNIA–BERKELEY
Berkeley, California

On Leap Year Day in 1976, a small group of people armed with buckets and paint scrapers climbed the steep path from the Greek Theater up Charter Hill. Their destination: the Big C. The group was made up of a few alumni and fifteen members of the Rally Committee from the University of California–Berkeley, led by Brad King, their chairman. The Rally Committee had been around since 1901, maintaining school traditions and the fun-loving spirit of the Cal Bears. Simply put, the Rally Committee were students who loved their school.

The old concrete C was covered in layers and layers of paint. Kneeling down, everyone pulled out their scrapers and began to scrape away the

43

1986 photo of the hillside letter that started it all, the Big C in Berkeley, California. The Big C represents the alma mater of the late James J. Parsons, professor of geography at the University of California–Berkeley, whose research on hillside letters makes him the "Father of Hillside Letters." —PHOTO BY JAMES J. PARSONS; COURTESY OF PAUL F. STARRS, UNIVERSITY OF NEVADA–RENO

paint, counting the coats as they peeled away the different colors. Finally, after about 120 coats, they came to the C's concrete surface. They were surprised to find in the lower arm of the letter the inscribed iron plate the sophomores had placed in the wet concrete back in 1905. For years it was assumed that the old iron plate had been removed and misplaced. To everyone's surprise, it was hidden under seventy-six years of paint. As the Rally Committee cleaned up the old plate, those who remembered recounted the story of the oldest hillside letter—the Big C.

For years prior to the building of the Big C, the freshman and sophomore classes had been competing to prove their superiority over each other, and as time went by their pranks had become violent. It began the afternoon before

Charter Day—the day the university celebrated its birthday—with the sophomore class custom of tying up any male freshmen they found. They tied them over fences, under bridges, or wherever they caught them. That evening the remaining freshman students would haul a barrel of white lime up Charter Hill and attempt to paint their class year on the hillside. The sophomores would respond by fighting their way up the hill in order to prevent this from happening and to attempt to paint their own class year instead. Charter Hill became a battleground, with students trying to drive off other students in a conflict they called Rushing. Some students were even seriously injured. The rivalry was so bad that the newspapers were reporting on it, and the alumni and state legislature were threatening to withhold funds from the university if the situation did not improve.

Because of the increasing violence, in 1905 the freshman and sophomore classes were pressured to call a truce, and they devised a plan. That year, instead of Rushing, the two classes decided to put their differences aside and join together to create a landmark for their school, a six-inch thick concrete C. They wanted to build it on their old battleground, Charter Hill. Some professors and local residents did not like the idea and immediately protested. They suggested a fountain, a bench, or a small bridge instead. One professor thought the classes should have a tug-of-war and take home pieces of rope as mementos. But the university president, Benjamin I. Wheeler, would have agreed to almost anything in order to see the end of Rushing, and he approved the students' plan. In two rain-soaked days, some two hundred young men built America's first hillside letter.

Upon completion of the C, the students placed in the lower arm of the letter the iron plate, which read, "In memory of the Rush, buried Charter Day 1905 by, Classes of 1907 and 1908, Requiescat in Pace" (Rest in Peace). The 1906 yearbook, *Blue and Gold*, commemorated the event with these words: "These two classes . . . will go down in the history of the University as those who sacrificed their class spirit for love of Alma Mater."

Freshman and sophomore men of UC Berkeley moved by hand the materials needed to construct the first hillside letter in the country in 1905. —UNIVERSITY OF CALIFORNIA–BERKELEY ARCHIVES

Students of UC–Berkeley guarding the Big C from attacks by their rival, Stanford, November 19, 1948. —UNIVERSITY OF CALIFORNIA–BERKELEY ARCHIVES

46

The Big C was immediately seized as a target by rival schools. In fact, this one-hundred-plus-year-old emblem has probably survived more attacks than any other hillside monogram. James Parsons, a professor at Berkeley who had an interest in hillside letters, wrote, "The first summer the C was damaged by dynamite, perhaps in one of the earliest instances of eco-radicalism."

Today the granddaddy of all hillside letters is still guarded by the Cal Bears Rally Committee when Berkeley plays Stanford. However, due to a grove of overgrown eucalyptus and Monterey pines, the school emblem is almost hidden from view. Yet the Big C continues to be hallowed in the school song:

On our rugged eastern foothills stands our symbol clear and bold
Big C means to fight and strive and win for the Blue and Gold.

	NAME	LOCATION	NOTE
CPP	Cal Poly Pomona	Pomona, CA	A CP was built for California State Polytechnic University–Pomona on Colt Hill in 1959 and was painted by the freshmen through the 1960s and 1970s; later, student groups took turns painting the letters their organization's colors. In 2004 the second P was added.
C	Calico Continuation High School	Yermo, CA	The rock C on Elephant Mountain represents the local high school. If you look to the northwest you can also see the word CALICO written in rocks above the old Calico ghost town.
CLU	California Lutheran University	Thousand Oaks, CA	In the early 1960s a rock CLC was built on Mount Clef by the students of Cal Lutheran College. It was lighted at night and used as a beacon by pilots flying into Los Angeles International Airport, until the energy crisis hit and the lights were turned off. When the school became a university in 1986, the second C was changed to a U. The "CLU Rocks" are painted each year by the freshman class during orientation week.
C	Cambridge	Cambridge, ID	Considered both a school and a community emblem, the C is painted by the senior class of Cambridge Junior-Senior High School. It is visible from U.S. 95.
C	Capitan High School	Capitan, NM	Maintained occasionally by the senior class.

47

	NAME	LOCATION	NOTE
C	Carlin	Carlin, NV	Featured on page 38.
C	Carroll College	Helena, MT	A rock C was removed.
C	Carson High School	Carson City, NV	Probably built sometime prior to 1925. Years ago, the student athletes supervised the whitewashing of the C by the freshmen and sophomores on Block C Day, and a picnic lunch on the mountain for the entire school followed. The C is still maintained.
C	Carter County High School	Ekalaka, MT	Northeast of town is a large metal C on a hillside the locals call C Hill. Each year the seniors paint the letter white and add their class year.
CG	Casa Grande	Casa Grande, AZ	The letters are maintained by the city parks and recreation department.
C	Cedar City High School	Cedar City, UT	Painted each year by the seniors and occasionally lighted.
C	Central High School	Anaconda, MT	First built in 1941 to represent Catholic Central School, which later changed its name to Central High School. The school closed in 1973, but the letter is still maintained occasionally by alumni.
C	Chadron State College	Chadron, NE	Featured on page 40.
C	Chaffey College	Rancho Cucamonga, CA	No longer maintained, overgrown with vegetation, and only visible from the air.
CMR	Charles M. Russell High School	Great Falls, MT	The high school decided not to maintain the monogram any longer and removed it.
C	Charlo High School	Charlo, MT	Painted biannually by the senior class.
C	Cimarron	Cimarron, NM	Fading and no longer maintained.
C	Clarkdale	Clarkdale, AZ	No longer cared for but still visible.
C	Clarkston High School	Clarkston, WA	Originally the C represented Charles Francis Adams High School, which later changed its name to Clarkston High School. In the 1930s the large white-washed rock C was capped by a rock bantam, the school mascot. The C is cared for by the senior class, which in 1996 started hauling up a few bags of concrete each year to stabilize the letter.
CV	Clearwater Valley High School	Kooskia, ID	First built in the 1960s, the rocks are whitewashed each year, and the seniors add below the CV their graduating year, which the juniors try to change to their year.
C	Clifton High School	Clifton, AZ	Maintained by the Clifton High Booster Club and lighted as part of the homecoming activities; visible along U.S. 191.

	NAME	LOCATION	NOTE
C	Coalinga	Coalinga, CA	No longer maintained but visible.
C	Cody High School	Cody, WY	Whitewashed annually by the senior class.
C	Coleville High School	Coleville, CA	Cared for and painted white by the students.
C	Colstrip	Colstrip, MT	Visible but not maintained.
C	Columbia University	New York, NY	The C was painted by the rowing team near the old boathouse on Manhattan's Harlem River, across from Lawrence Wien Stadium.
C	Colville High School	Colville, WA	Years ago the C Club of Colville High School maintained this letter, visible along U.S. 395. The community has placed a lighted cross directly above the letter.
CHS	Condon High School	Condon, OR	The rock letters are painted red, white, and blue; nearby is an American flag made of painted rocks.
C	Coolidge High School	Coolidge, AZ	Located on Walker Butte, the C is maintained by the students and visible along Route 387.
C	Coronado High School	El Paso, TX	One of six hillside letters in El Paso, five of which are high school letters. The C is no longer maintained but is visible.
C	Corvallis High School	Corvallis, MT	Maintained annually by the senior class.
C	Costilla	Costilla, NM	Featured on page 42.
C	Cottonwood	Cottonwood, AZ	This community on Route 89 in central Arizona has a C that is maintained by various service organizations.
C	Crane	Crane, OR	Community letter cared for by the students of Crane Union High School.
C	Culver High School	Culver, OR	Maintained by the students on the football team.
C	University of California–Berkeley	Berkeley, CA	Featured on page 43.
C	University of California–Riverside	Riverside, CA	Built on Box Springs Mountain in August 1955 by university students and painted by the freshmen. Students did the surveying and E. L. Yeager Construction Company provided the cement. At 132 feet long, it is more than four times larger than its granddaddy, the Big C at the Berkeley campus.
CU	University of Colorado–Boulder	Boulder, CO	If you look carefully you can see where two mystery letters were once painted on the northernmost face of the Flatiron Mountains overlooking Boulder. Some think the emblem was a DU for Denver University or a UO for the University of Oklahoma (University of Colorado's rival), but most say it was a CU.

D DIXIE HIGH SCHOOL AND
DIXIE STATE COLLEGE OF UTAH
St. George, Utah

The whitewashed rock D on the Black Hill, which stood for Dixie High Academy, stands out prominently on the west side of St. George. The D has a history linked with that of the word DIXIE that is painted across the Sugar Loaf, a rounded rock outcropping along the Red Hill just to the north of town.

The story behind how this rapidly growing southern Utah community got the nickname "Dixie" dates back to the Civil War. St. George had been founded in 1854 by Brigham Young, the leader of the Mormon Church. Young believed it might become necessary for the early settlers of Utah to grow their own cotton because of the war, so he sent new church converts, many originally from the southern states, to St. George to begin a "cotton mission." These southern settlers began referring to the area as "Utah's Dixie," and when the first secondary school opened in 1912, it was named Dixie High Academy.

The rivalry between classes at Dixie High Academy was intense in those first few years, and it worsened when students of the class of 1913 painted a large white D and their graduating year on the red sandstone face of the Sugar Loaf rock. The class of 1914 immediately reacted and within days had obliterated the number 3 with red paint and painted a white 4 in its place. This exchange of numbers occurred every few days. "In fact," wrote Matthew Bentley, who was a student at the school during this time and later became

The only structure on the Black Hill in St. George back in 1915 was the giant rock D built by students of Dixie High Academy. Today the D is surrounded by homes and businesses in this rapidly growing community.
—PHOTO BY JACOB KING

president of Dixie State College, "it became customary to look toward the Sugar Loaf every morning to see who had taken the night shift. The change of ownership was not bad in itself, but there were often bare-fisted encounters before it was determined which class would be represented with numerals greeting the public."

After the class of 1913 graduated, the class of 1915 took up the challenge with their own numerals. The encounters continued until the spring of 1914, when a real knock-down drag-out fight occurred between the classes of 1914 and 1915. Following this large, unruly encounter, the school and student body officers met to discuss how to end the escalating rivalry. Their solution: the boys of the academy would replace the D and class year on the Sugar Loaf with the painted word DIXIE, and the school and townspeople would build a rock D on the face of the Black Hill.

These two plans seemed to redirect the energy of both classes from robust rivalry to productive projects. Soon after school began in the fall of 1914, Leo A. Snow, a young civil engineer living in St. George, surveyed and laid out the border of the rock D. The dimensions were 75 feet across and 100 feet long. The actual construction was completed by male students, faculty, and townspeople, with the female students and ladies of the community arriving around noon with wagons loaded with food. After the picnic lunch, a short program followed that included remarks from the school administration and some prominent community and church leaders.

Male members of Dixie High Academy's class of 1914 are ready to protect their hand-painted insignia on the Sugar Loaf. This emblem is now maintained by the students of Dixie High School.
—COURTESY OF VAL A. BROWNING LIBRARY, DIXIE STATE COLLEGE OF UTAH

This painted emblem was created to end the growing rivalry between the classes of Dixie High Academy.
—PHOTO BY KEN SNOW

Dixie High Academy later became Dixie State College of Utah. Today the built-up D is maintained by the students of Dixie State College during the school's annual D Week celebration (see photo on page 7), and the painted DIXIE is looked after by the students of Dixie High School.

D **DUARTE**
Duarte, California

Most hillside emblems are simple block letters that represent the name of a school or a community, but the D that overlooks the community of Duarte, California, a few miles east of Pasadena, is a stylized insignia of great historical significance.

During the 1830s, when California was part of the northern region of Mexico called Alta California, Andres Duarte, a corporal in the Mexican army, was assigned to keep watch over the land from San Gabriel Mission to San Bernardino. Duarte enjoyed his assignment and quickly grew to love the lush land of the upper San Gabriel Valley and the Rio Azusa (San Gabriel River) that flowed through it.

Upon retirement, Duarte was granted a pension of nearly seven thousand acres of land from the governor of Alta California. Duarte and his family established a ranch they named Rancho Azusa de Duarte and built a small adobe home. With help from some of the local Indians, Duarte planted crops and raised livestock with his wife, Gertrude, and their son, Felipe Santiago. Unfortunately, Duarte lost his ranch some years later because he was unable to pay the back taxes levied upon him after the end of the Mexican-American War in 1848. But the city has not forgotten Duarte's love for this valley. Over one hundred years after Duarte had designed a D to brand his cattle, the city of Duarte used that design in their city seal and flag.

53

In 1979 a large subdivision of homes was built in Duarte. As part of the contract, the city had asked the developer to construct Andres Duarte's brand on a hill overlooking the development. Originally, Duarte's D was made of shrubbery outlined with concrete. During the 1990s, however, because of the constant maintenance required, the city removed the vegetation and filled in the area with concrete. They painted the D white and added lights. The city lighted their D for about three years, until the lights were removed due to complaints by some of the locals.

The D can be seen south of Interstate 210 and west of Interstate 605. A replica of Andres Duarte's branding iron is at the Duarte Historical Museum, where you can learn more about the unique history of the San Gabriel Valley and Duarte, California.

The hillside emblem of Duarte, California, is a reproduction of the branding iron designed by Andres Duarte, who settled in the valley when it was part of Mexico. —PHOTO BY ALAN M. HELLER

INSET: A replica of Duarte's branding iron. —PHOTO BY ALAN HELLER; COURTESY OF THE DUARTE HISTORICAL MUSEUM

	NAME	LOCATION	NOTE
D	The Dalles High School	The Dalles, OR	Formerly painted by the letterman club of the old The Dalles High School, the D is no longer maintained but is still visible.
D	Dawson County High School	Glendive, MT	Maintained by the students.
D	Dayton	Dayton, NV	Whitewashed rock letter maintained by the townspeople.
D	Deary High School	Deary, ID	The D is painted white and is invisible in the winter when snow camouflages it.
D	Del Norte	Del Norte, CO	Represents both Del Norte High School and the community; maintained by the school.
D	Denton	Denton, MT	Representing both the community and Denton High School, the concrete D is painted annually by the seniors.
D	Dilcon/Dilkon	Dilcon, AZ	Dilcon, AZ, derived its name from the Navajo word dilkon, which means "smooth black rock" or "bare surface." Overlooking the Dilcon Community School is a large smooth rock with a white D painted on it. Overlooking the town on a different hill, the students of the Dilcon Community School painted the name of their town, spelling it DILKON.
D	Dinuba High School	Dinuba, CA	The white concrete D often becomes a red O when altered by the students of Orosi High School, Dinuba's rival.
DIXIE	Dixie High School	St. George, UT	Featured on page 50.
D	Dixie State College of Utah	St. George, UT	Featured on page 50. See also photo on page 7.
D	Dons of West Las Vegas High School	Las Vegas, NM	Stands for the Dons, the school mascot; maintained by the students.
D	Douglas High School	Douglas, AZ	The boys of Douglas High School built the 100-foot-tall D in 1933 to show their school spirit; it is still maintained and lighted by the school.
D	Douglas High School	Minden, NV	Cared for by the students.
D	Drummond High School	Drummond, MT	Maintained annually by the seniors or student council.
D	Duarte	Duarte, CA	Featured on page 53.
D	Duchesne High School	Duchesne, UT	Maintained by the seniors; visible north of Route 40.
D	Duncan High School	Duncan, AZ	Maintained by the school maintenance crew.

E ELKO
Elko, Nevada

On October 2, 1916, the citizens of Elko, Nevada, were saddened to read the headline of their local newspaper, the *Elko Free Press*: "Elko High School Teacher Dies in Ruby Mountains from Exposure in Storm." The death of Raymond Thomas, the young physical education teacher at Elko High School, initiated the building of the 120-foot-wide, 204-foot-long E in Elko.

Thomas, an avid hiker, was one of a group of ten people from town who had organized a camping and climbing trip into the nearby Ruby Mountains. The group included seven schoolteachers, two eighth-grade students, and a book-keeper.

On the first morning of their hike the group split up, with Thomas and a few others hoping to hike a little higher to some waterfalls. Within hours, however, Thomas's group encountered an unexpected torrential rainstorm. Temperatures quickly dropped and everyone was soaked. Thomas headed back alone for help, but collapsed along the trail due to hypothermia. The rest of the party was eventually rescued, but Thomas died a day later.

As a tribute to their teacher, the boys from Elko High School decided to build a hillside emblem to honor Thomas. They cleared an area on the hillside above Elko, and then they moved—by hand—thousands of rocks to form the built-up E.

This letter was painted and maintained for years by the students of Elko High School, and as time went on the E became an important landmark in the

The E in Elko, Nevada, was built in 1916, making it the oldest high school letter in the country. —PHOTO BY HOWARD HICKSON, ELKO, NEVADA

community. Nearly a century old, the E is now maintained by the Veterans of Foreign Wars Post 2350. Each year for Christmas and Easter a lighted cross is superimposed on the E for about tens days to celebrate the holidays.

In the nearby Ruby Mountains is Thomas Canyon, named after the young schoolteacher who died trying to save the lives of his friends and became the inspiration for Elko's E.

E ESCALANTE
Escalante, Utah

Whitewashed volcanic rocks form the E northeast of Escalante, Utah, which was settled by Mormon pioneers in 1876. This scenic town is surrounded by some of the most remote wilderness country in the United States, including the Grand Staircase–Escalante National Monument to the south.

The whitewashed E is an important landmark to the small community of Escalante, Utah, in the heart of southern Utah. —PHOTO BY JIM CORNING

One of the most popular hikes in the monument is along the old mail trail. Until 1942, mules carried the mail between the communities of Escalante and Boulder. The mail carriers would climb the steep, rocky trail past the whitewashed E with mail stuffed in canvas pouches on the backs of their mules. On the way back from Boulder, along with the mail the mules would often carry cans filled with cream headed for the creamery. The old mail trail was so rough that by the time the mules had reached the E, the cream had been churned to butter—or so say the old-timers in town.

Escalante High School students and teachers built the E in 1926 to commemorate their first high school building. For many years each spring on E Day, the freshmen or sophomores would spend the day whitewashing the E. That night they would hike back up to the letter to light it.

The trail to the E was so treacherous that in 1961 the students set up a temporary E on the Big Hill just west of town, where lighting the letter would be easier. To light the new E the students would place old jeans, which they collected from the townsfolk, into metal cans filled with fuel, and then they would line them up to form the letter E. The lighted jeans would burn far into the night. Today, the original rock E remains, and the students of Escalante High School still celebrate E Day annually by lighting a second E on the Big Hill for one night.

	NAME	LOCATION	NOTE
EC	El Capitan High School	Lakeside, CA	Cared for by the students.
E	El Paso High School	El Paso, TX	The students lighted the E during their homecoming football game until the 1980s, when the city began giving citations for such activities. Now for homecoming they light luminaries in the shape of an E on the football field and turn out the lights.
E	El Rito Elementary School	El Rito, NM	Originally an N for El Rito Normal School, the letter was made into an E by the El Rito Elementary School students, who continue to maintain it. It is one of the few letters representing an elementary school.
E	Eldorado High School	Las Vegas, NV	The E was built in 1978 after three years of opposition and controversy.
E	Elko	Elko, NV	Featured on page 56.
E	Elsinore	Elsinore, UT	The whitewashed rock E is maintained by the townspeople.
E	Ennis High School	Ennis, MT	Painted annually by the student council.
E	Enterprise High School	Enterprise, UT	The rock E was built on a volcano cone and is maintained by the students.
E	Escalante	Escalante, UT	Featured on page 57.
E	Eureka High School	Eureka, NV	Built during the 1960s; painted yearly on E-day by the students.
E	Evanston	Evanston, WY	A community letter maintained by the city.

F FLORENCE
Florence, Arizona

If you think you are hallucinating in the heat of the Arizona desert, you're not. Located on Poston Butte just north of Florence, Arizona, there is not only a hillside letter F, but also a pyramid. Buried beneath the pyramid are the remains of Charles DeBrille Poston, who was the first delegate to Congress from the Arizona Territory and became known as the Father of Arizona.

Poston was one of the driving forces behind making a territory of the untamed lands of Arizona. He was known for his eloquence in speaking and writing, and when Congress heard him expound on the mineral wealth in Arizona they began to listen, because the government, as usual, was in need of money. Poston knew what he was talking about; he owned one of the first silver mines in the area. In fact, when President Lincoln signed the document creating the Arizona Territory on February 24, 1863, Poston presented Lincoln with a silver inkstand made from his own silver.

Poston was eccentric and loved to delve into studies of the exotic and the occult. He traveled to the Far East and got involved with Zoroastrianism, an ancient religion that uses fire as a divine symbol. Poston was fascinated by the rubble of an old stone tower that American Indians had once used as a lookout atop Primrose Hill. He believed this tower was part of an ancient temple site where the Indians worshiped a sun god.

Poston eventually spent thousands of dollars of his fortune to build a road to the top of the hill, where he would stay for days at a time. It was Poston's

Poston Butte, also called F Mountain, in Florence, Arizona. —PHOTO BY JIM CORNING

wish to build upon the hill a temple with an eternal flame and to be buried
there. Unfortunately, Poston died in poverty in 1902 and was buried in a pau-
pers' field in Phoenix. In 1925 the state of Arizona built a pyramid of mortared
cobblestone atop the butte Poston loved so much. His body was transferred in
a metal casket and buried beneath the pyramid.

The rock F located on the south face of the butte was most likely constructed
by students in Florence during the 1920s, shortly after the first high school
was built in 1919. In the beginning, the freshman class regularly painted the
F, walking up the back side of the butte on the very road Poston had built for
his buckboard wagon. Today the locals call Poston's resting place F Mountain.
The F is still maintained, most recently by some of the prisoners from a state
prison complex on the outskirts of town.

If you are ever traveling along Arizona 79 north of Florence, you can stop and climb up Poston's buckboard road on the back side of F Mountain. When you reach the top of the butte, you will see not only the valley that entranced Poston but also the hometown landmark of Florence, Arizona.

The pyramid atop F Mountain outside of Florence, Arizona, houses the remains of Charles DeBrille Poston, the "Father of Arizona." —PHOTO BY JIM CORNING

	NAME	LOCATION	NOTE
F	Fallon	Fallon, NV	A community letter made of rocks and painted white; maintained by the city.
FHS	Fernley High School	Fernley, NV	First built as a single letter F in about 1981, with the HS added later; it is visible but not maintained.
F	Fillmore High School	Fillmore, CA	Maintained by the students.
F	Flathead High School	Kalispell, MT	Built by the students about 1926, the F used to be painted and lighted by the freshman class; today it is maintained by the students.
F	Florence	Florence, AZ	Featured on page 60.
F	Forsyth	Forsyth, MT	The F was originally built by the students of Forsyth High School, but the townspeople are not quite sure when. It is located on private land where the owner cares for this community letter.
FB	Fort Benton High School	Fort Benton, MT	Maintained by the senior class.
FD	Fort Davis High School	Fort Davis, TX	The whitewashed rock letters have been maintained by the seniors.
FG	Fountain Green	Fountain Green, UT	A community letter built in 2001 as Justin Aagard's Eagle Scout project.
F	Frazer High School	Frazer, MT	The F is painted by the seniors, who add their class year below it.
F	Fredonia High School	Fredonia, AZ	Maintained annually by the students.
F	Frenchtown High School	Frenchtown, MT	Constructed of concrete by students in 2005, replacing the old rock letter that had been there for decades; it is painted white by the students and is visible north of Interstate 90.
F	Fromberg High School	Fromberg, MT	Painted by the freshmen as part of their high school initiation.

G GARIBALDI
Garibaldi, Oregon

A hillside G has stood watch over the coastal community of Garibaldi, Oregon, and the Tillamook Bay for nearly three quarters of a century. It was built due to the enthusiasm and efforts of two boys, Bill White and Roy Albers, from Garibaldi High School. In 1929, White and Albers were part of a small group of students who had dreams of going to college someday. Their principal, J. E. O'Neel, was taking the two boys and a few other students to Corvallis, Oregon, to check out Oregon Agriculture College (now Oregon State University). As they were traveling, they passed by a hillside A near Amity, Oregon, and began to consider the possibility of making a G for Garibaldi.

Back at school, the group shared the idea with the other students, but no one else seemed interested. Roy Albers, however, could not contain his eagerness and brought the matter before the next student council, which approved the idea. Albers and White were put in charge of selecting the site and designing the letter. White consulted Otto Schrader, the plant engineer for the Hammond Tillamook Lumber Company, who advised White about constructing the letter. Based on Schrader's advice, White created the design for the G, and the lumber company donated shiplap boards and two-by-fours for the project.

Next, White and Albers had to tackle the problem of laying out the G on a sloping surface in such a way that it would appear straight regardless of the viewing angle. With boyhood ingenuity, the two young men borrowed bedsheets from home and headed up the steep slope above town. They selected a site and tied two ends of a bedsheet to stakes, one above the other. Then Albers left the hill to station himself about a mile away. Using a long pole with another bedsheet attached, Albers signaled to White which direction to move the lower stake to make the sheet on the hill appear vertical.

By the spring of 1930, the school's student body and faculty, along with some townspeople, completed a built-up wooden G that was 32 feet wide and 40 feet long. The new community landmark became known as the Big G. A bench was placed at the top of the G so hikers could rest and enjoy the spectacular view, and a fire line was cut around the G to protect it. However, the

The Big G overlooking Garibaldi, Oregon, is a beloved landmark of the small coastal community. Built around eighty years ago, it is lighted at night and serves as a beacon to boats entering the bay. —PHOTO BY CAROLEE NORTH

original G was lost two years later as a result of a forest fire. Before the first G was destroyed, Doctor E. R. Huckleberry, the local physician, said that one summer, using field glasses from the back of his office, he watched a bear climb onto the G each afternoon for "a cozy nap." Huckleberry surmised that the surface of the G got quite warm in the afternoon sun and made an inviting place for the bear to sleep.

The school constructed a second wooden G the year after the fire. This second G remained for over forty years, until 1972, when the Garibaldi Fire Department rebuilt it of corrugated metal painted white. Shortly after this G was built, the community raised enough money to add lights to this hillside letter. In the beginning the G was lighted only for special occasions, and then eventually the community kept the lights on all year long, even changing them from white to red for the holidays.

The lighted G stood over Tillamook Bay for well over three decades, acting as a beacon for boats coming into the harbor. Then in 1999, after vandals had waged repeated attacks on the light bulbs, the community shut off the lights of its hometown landmark. A group of citizen volunteers, many of whom had cared for the G since high school, officially formed the Friends of the Big G and went to work finding vandal-proof fixtures to replace the old lights. The group raised over four thousand dollars, and by October 1999 the lights were back on, safely guiding boats into the harbor.

G GRAND COUNTY HIGH SCHOOL
Moab, Utah

In 1924, a group of high school seniors painted a white letter G on the red cliffs overlooking Moab, Utah, which sits on the banks of the Colorado River between Arches and Canyonlands National Parks. They wanted the painted letter to be their legacy to future graduating classes of Grand County High

The Big G was painted on the red sandstone hills overlooking Moab, Utah, for Grand County High School in 1924.
—PHOTO BY TOM TAYLOR

School. Over thirty feet long, this emblem can be seen downtown along the northeast side of the Moab ridge and is referred to by locals as the Big G.

One summer morning in 2000, the residents of Moab woke to find the seventy-six-year-old emblem gone. Someone had painted over it during the night in a color that made it invisible against the red cliffs. A number of people contributed money to be used as a reward to find the culprits. Most of the old-timers blamed it on environmentalists who were newer residents of town, but no one knows for sure who did it. Many people wrote emotional letters, both pro and con, to the editor of the local paper over whether the Big G should be restored. The controversy ended as abruptly as it started when Davy Stewart and Guy Johnston, alumni of Grand County High School, rappelled over the towering red cliffs and repainted the Big G, using materials donated by local businesses (see photo on page 17).

Davy Stewart has pledged he will continue to care for this hometown landmark as long as he can. The mystery of the disappearance of the Big G has never been resolved, and neither has the controversy over the letter.

	NAME	LOCATION	NOTE
G	Gabbs High School	Gabbs, NV	Originally a T built by the students in 1954, when the town and school were named Toiyabe. When the name was changed to Gabbs in 1956 it became a G.
G	Galena High School	Reno, NV	Maintained annually by the student government.
GHS	Ganado High School	Ganado, AZ	Built and maintained by the high school.
G	Gap	Gap, AZ	This small Navajo community has painted a G near the top of a beautiful sandstone mountain near Cameron. The G is difficult to spot; it can best be seen between mile markers 498 and 499 on U.S. 89. See photo on page 9.
G	Gardiner High School	Gardiner, MT	Whitewashed and maintained annually by the senior class.
G	Garibaldi	Garibaldi, OR	Featured on page 64.
G	Geraldine	Geraldine, MT	A community letter maintained by the Geraldine High School Letterman Club.
G	Geyser High School	Geyser, MT	Maintained annually by the seniors and freshmen; visible along U.S. 87.
G	Glenwood	Glenwood, UT	Built in 2003 by the family members of Archibald T. Oldroyd, the founder of Glenwood, as part of their family reunion.
G	Globe High School	Globe, AZ	The G is painted green by the high school freshmen but is sometimes blackened with tar by students from nearby Miami, Arizona.
G	Goldendale High School	Goldendale, WA	Maintained by the school and lighted for homecoming; visible south of U.S. 97.

	NAME	LOCATION	NOTE
G	Grand County High School	Moab, UT	Featured on page 66. See also photo on page 17.
G	Granite High School	Philipsburg, MT	A rock letter painted each year by the seniors as part of their homecoming activities.
G	Grants High School	Grants, NM	Painted on the face of a red mesa, usually by school alumni because of liability issues.
GR	Grass Range	Grass Range, MT	Maintained by groups in the community.
GF	Great Falls	Great Falls, MT	The GF stands for the town and is maintained by the community.
G	Green River	Green River, UT	A community letter cared for by the townspeople; visible south of Interstate 70.
GR	Green River	Green River, WY	A community letter maintained by the city.
G	Greybull	Greybull, WY	During the 1960s it was an annual tradition that the freshmen of Greybull High School, wearing diapers over their clothes, had to pull the seniors in small wagons up the hillside to the G, where the seniors directed its white-washing. In 2005 the parents of the senior class painted the G blue. It can be seen along U.S. 14.
G	Grossmont High School	El Cajon, CA	Painted blue and gold, the school colors.
G	Guernsey-Sunrise High School	Guernsey, WY	Removed in 2005 when the land ownership changed hands.
G	Gunnison High School	Gunnison, CO	Built in 1915, the G on Smelter Hill was originally an N for Colorado State Normal School, which changed its name to Western State College in 1923 and gave the letter to Gunnison High School. The high school changed the letter to a G, which is no longer painted; however, the junior class lights the letter each year for homecoming.
G	Gunnison Valley High School	Gunnison, UT	Once a year the freshmen spend the day doing community service and painting their G.

H BLACK HILLS STATE UNIVERSITY
Spearfish, South Dakota

Each year, millions of people visit Mount Rushmore in the Black Hills of South Dakota to see the enormous faces of four of our United States presidents carved in stone. Visitors to the Black Hills with an interest in giant landmarks might also want to see the letter H located in Spearfish, South Dakota, the home of Black Hills State University, just seventy miles north of Mount Rushmore. The H can be viewed almost anywhere in Spearfish by looking east toward Lookout Mountain.

The Yellow Jacket is the mascot of Black Hills State University, and homecoming is called Swarm Day. In 1955, Bob Temple, the student body president, wanted to add some spirit to the traditional homecoming activities, which until then had consisted of a parade, a football game, and a dance. He proposed building a hillside H, which stands for Hills and is the letter students receive for lettering in athletics. Temple and other students thought that Lookout Mountain, one of the three prominent mountains around Spearfish, was the best choice. Many community residents disagreed, feeling that the H would deface the mountain, especially after the school newspaper, the *Anemone*, published a photograph of Lookout Mountain with an H drawn in the center of it.

The school's president, Russell Jonas, quickly created a committee to consider the issue that was dividing the students and the community. He stated

The H for Black Hills State University in Spearfish, South Dakota, is one of only two hillside letters in the state. —PHOTO BY CONNIE HANSEN, BLACK HILLS STATE UNIVERSITY

in the *Queen City Mail*, the local newspaper, that perhaps there had been a misunderstanding as to the exact location of the H. In January 1956, the matter escalated again when a group of enterprising students spread lime on the hillside in the form of a giant H. The committee stepped in and convinced the parties that the H should be moved to a more "discrete" location along the northern part of Lookout Mountain, where Josef Meier, a local landowner, had offered his property for the letter. Both parties agreed.

In the summer of 1956 the school hired three students, Jim Brown, Herman Boner, and Bob Clithero, to construct the H. They began by building a giant wooden form in the shape of the letter. The face of Lookout Mountain was so steep at that particular location that the cement truck had to drive up the back of the mountain to deliver the concrete. Then, using handcarts to haul the concrete, the three young men filled the form.

For the next few years, the freshmen whitewashed the concrete H as part of their initiation activities before Swarm Day. After pouring the lime mixture on the steep H, they slid down it, using their bodies to do the whitewashing. In the late 1970s the freshmen accidentally purchased the wrong kind of lime, and over a hundred students received chemical burns. Since then, the H is no longer whitewashed, but it is still very visible. The H in Spearfish is one of only two hillside letters in the state of South Dakota.

	NAME	LOCATION	NOTE
H	Black Hills State University	Spearfish, SD	Featured on page 70.
H	Hamilton High School	Hamilton, MT	The senior class whitewashes and cares for the H.
H	Harlowton High School	Harlowton, MT	Painted during homecoming week by the sophomores.
H	Harper High School	Harper, OR	Made of chalk rock and maintained by the seniors.
H	Hartville	Hartville, WY	The H is a community letter. There are no schools left in Hartville, but whenever alumni come back for a reunion they repaint their old hillside emblem.
H	Havre High School	Havre, MT	There are two Hs in Havre, both considered high school letters. One is located along Bullhook Road and is no longer cared for by the students; however, the school still maintains the wooden H near the football field.
H	Hawthorne	Hawthorne, NV	A community letter cared for by the townspeople.
H	Hayden High School	Hayden, AZ	The seniors of Hayden High School, located two miles away in Winkelman, paint their letter and add their class year.
H	Hazen	Hazen, NV	The rock H is a community letter and is maintained.

	NAME	LOCATION	NOTE
H	Helena	Helena, MT	Originally the emblem of Helena High School, the H was maintained by the H Club; the school has turned the letter and its maintenance over to the city.
H	Hellgate High School	Missoula, MT	Removed.
H	Henley High School	Klamath Falls, OR	A rock letter maintained by the school; any student can volunteer to paint it.
H	Herbert Hoover High School	Glendale, CA	No longer maintained by the school.
H	Highland High School	Salt Lake City, UT	A white letter with a black background on a small mountain face, the H was first painted shortly after the school opened in the 1960s.
H	Highwood High School	Highwood, MT	The rock H located behind the school is painted white by the freshmen and sophomores the first week of school in the fall. The letter used to be whitewashed by freshmen dressed in diapers and construction boots.
H	Hinsdale High School	Hinsdale, MT	The school's H is made of railroad ties, and its maintenance is the responsibility of each new freshman class.
H	Holbrook High School	Holbrook, AZ	Removed.
H	Hondo High School	Hondo, NM	The H is maintained by the seniors, who add their class year beside it.
H	Hornbrook Elementary School	Hornbrook, CA	Maintained by the eighth-graders.
H	Horseshoe Bend	Horseshoe Bend, ID	The H was made of tin in 1977 by the high school shop class of Horseshoe Bend School, which includes students K through 12. It is considered both a school and a community letter.
H	Hot Springs High School	Hot Springs, MT	Cared for by members of the senior class.
H	Hotchkiss	Hotchkiss, CO	Believed to have been built during the 1950s, it represents both the community and Hotchkiss High School and continues to be maintained.
H	Huntington	Huntington, OR	Visible but no longer maintained.
H	Hurricane High School	Hurricane, UT	Built in 1925 to celebrate the community's first high school.
H	New Mexico Highlands University	Las Vegas, NM	What was first an N for New Mexico Normal School was later changed to an H when the school became New Mexico Highlands University. Various student groups from the university maintain the H.

I IDAHO STATE UNIVERSITY
Pocatello, Idaho

Some hillside monograms transform from one letter to another. Such was the case at Idaho State University in southeastern Idaho. In 1916, after the Academy of Idaho in Pocatello became Idaho Technical Institute, some students wanted to put an "imperishable token" on Red Hill. They asked that a special assembly be held. The student body president, Roy J. Logan, conducted the assembly and requested funds to construct an emblem on the hill. In less than twenty minutes, they collected enough funds from the students and faculty in attendance to build the letter.

That very afternoon the entire student body and faculty gathered up every available shovel, pick, and hoe and headed for Red Hill. Effie Swanson Fugate, a student at the time, later told how she struggled up the hill, with her long skirts tucked in her bloomers, and used a hoe to help form the school's first emblem, a rock T for Idaho Technical Institute.

The T remained on the hill overlooking campus for the next ten years. Then in 1925, southeastern Idahoans and President Charles R. Frazier of Idaho Technical Institute asked the Idaho state legislature to turn ITI into a four-year school, in order to give the students in southern Idaho the same educational opportunities that students in northern Idaho had. Unfortunately, the state house and senate defeated the measure by a total of only four votes, and the Idaho State Board of Education dismissed Frazier for his connection with the movement.

To prevent the giant I of Idaho State University from sliding off Red Hill, drainage pipes have been installed to allow the runoff water to flow beneath the rock and concrete emblem.

—PHOTO BY JAMES J. PARSONS; COURTESY OF PAUL F. STARRS, UNIVERSITY OF NEVADA–RENO

After this, ITI students decided to take matters in their own hands. Former student Herb Fritz remembers that nearly a hundred men, using the light of small bonfires, spent a night tirelessly working with picks and shovels and whitewash, turning the rock T into the number 4. The next morning, a resolution was read throughout the campus, stating:

> We, members of the student body of the Tech hereby band ourselves together and resolve that we will fearlessly do whatever lies in our power to further any action that will secure a four-year degree-granting college for southern Idaho. It is also resolved, that we have been informed that the huge 'T' on the hills overlooking the campus has by the diligent work of students and townspeople been altered until it resembles a gigantic '4.' It is resolved that this '4' as constructed shall remain permanently in place until such time as a four year course has been secured for the Idaho Institute.

Unfortunately for the students, the 4 on the hill faded away with the winter snows, leaving only the structure of the T for the students to patiently continue to whitewash.

In 1927, Idaho lawmakers compromised: they wouldn't make ITI a four-year college, but they would make it a branch of the University of Idaho–Moscow and would give the school a new name—University of Idaho, Southern Branch. The students celebrated this name change by removing the arms of the old rock T and making the letter an I.

Twenty years later, the movement begun by southeastern Idahoans, Frazier, and the students of ITI paid off. In 1947 the legislature approved a four-year program and renamed the institution Idaho State College. It became Idaho State University in 1963, and the hillside I in Pocatello has remained on Red Hill southeast of town to the present day.

I INTERMOUNTAIN INTER-TRIBAL INDIAN SCHOOL
Brigham City, Utah

The painted I on a hillside near Brigham City, Utah, represents the Intermountain Inter-tribal Indian School. First known as the Intermountain Indian School, it opened its doors in January 1950 in an old abandoned army hospital. Over five hundred Indian students, from elementary to high school level, were bused from Arizona that first year to attend the boarding school.

The school in Brigham City was different from most other Indian boarding schools of the time because in addition to being taught academic subjects, the students were able to learn about their own culture and language. At first, students came only from the Navajo tribe. By the late 1970s enrollment was down, and the school changed its name to Intermountain Inter-tribal Indian

The Intermountain Inter-tribal Indian School, which has been closed for more than twenty years, sits below its hillside I.
—PHOTO BY CINDY HENRY

School and began accepting students from nearly a hundred tribes from all over the nation.

During the 1970s, the students painted a huge white I on a rocky slope overlooking their school. By the 1980s the Bureau of Indian Affairs began closing many Indian boarding schools, favoring instead local schools on the Indian reservations. One of the last boarding schools to be closed was the Intermountain Inter-tribal Indian School, in 1984.

As the years passed, the I began to fade. Then at a 1998 school reunion, former students and teachers decided the I needed a new coat of paint. With buckets of whitewash, alumni of the Indian School repainted the fading hillside emblem. The I is still there, a reminder of a time when many Native American children had to leave their homes and families to go to school. Parts of the old school remain, and some of the buildings now house local businesses.

	NAME	LOCATION	NOTE
I	Idaho State University	Pocatello, ID	Featured on page 74.
IS	Indian Springs High School	Indian Springs, NV	The IS was built in the late 1960s to commemorate the town's first high school; it is cared for by school alumni and the community.
I	Intermountain Inter-tribal Indian School	Brigham City, UT	Featured on page 76.
I	Ione High School	Ione, OR	Maintained annually by the senior class.
I	Iraan High School	Iraan, TX	Lighted continually during the entire school year.

J JEFFERSON HIGH SCHOOL
Boulder, Montana

Boulder, Montana, the seat of Jefferson County in the west-central part of the state, is home to a rock letter J. Boulder got its name from the huge rocks that are scattered about the valley. Students of what used to be called Jefferson County High School used thousands of the smaller boulders to build their school emblem on the Depot Hill, just northeast of town.

The whitewashed rock J, which stands for Jefferson High School, has overlooked the quiet town of Boulder, Montana, for around eighty years. —PHOTO BY CODY E. RICHARDSON

79

As to the date the J was built, even the older townsfolk aren't sure, but it was probably around 1927. The students would maintain the J by taking a day off from school to whitewash it. They would bring old brooms from home, and the school would provide the whitewash. This tradition is much the same today. Now it is the senior class at Jefferson High School that whitewashes the rock J as part of its homecoming festivities. Like hundreds of students before them for the past eighty years, class members often return from this activity more covered in whitewash than the rocks and boulders that compose the J.

	NAME	LOCATION	NOTE
J	Jackson Elementary School	Jackson, MT	Jackson is a small town with no high school, so the elementary school children maintain their J. A local farmer made the J of iron so it would last, and the children paint it white.
J	Jefferson High School	Boulder, MT	Featured on page 79.
J	Jefferson High School	El Paso, TX	The whitewashed rock J is no longer maintained by the school and is fading.
J	Jerome	Jerome, AZ	The old mining community of Jerome no longer has any schools, but the townsfolk in Jerome and surrounding areas formed a J Club, which maintains the J and performs other community service projects.
J	Joliet	Joliet, MT	Represents both Joliet High School and the community; painted by the students.
J	Jordan	Jordan, MT	A community letter maintained annually by the students of Garfield County District High School.
JV	Jordan Valley	Jordan Valley, OR	No longer maintained but still visible.
JC	Joseph City	Joseph City, AZ	The hillside JC is cared for by the community.
J	Juab High School	Nephi, UT	Represents the third oldest high school in Utah; students paint and light the J annually.
J	St. Joseph College	Albuquerque, NM	Students of St. Joseph College, now closed, painted a J on Vulcan Volcano before it became part of Petroglyph National Monument. The letter was whitewashed and maintained into the early 1960s; later Albuquerque's Open Space Task Division tried to restore the area by painting over the whitewashed J to camouflage it. However, the J seems to be reappearing as the dark paint wears off.

K **KANAB**
Kanab, Utah

Kanab, Utah, is nicknamed "Utah's Little Hollywood" because its picturesque sandstone and sagebrush landscape has for many years been a popular backdrop for movies. Kanab has a hillside letter with a history about as long as that of the silver screen. Sometime in the early 1920s, the students of the old Kanab High School on Main Street built and whitewashed a rock K near the school. The K was a community and school landmark for nearly eighty years. Then in 2003, the metal sheets that formed the K were torn off the hillside during a windstorm and were not restored.

In 2005, fifteen-year-old Brett Jackson was looking for an Eagle Scout project. His father, Stan Jackson, encouraged Brett to select a project that would last. Brett knew many of Kanab's residents missed the old K, so he decided that for his project he would rebuild the K for the community. With the help of his father and others who donated labor and materials, Brett built a wooden K, painted it white, and fashioned it to a metal frame. The new K weighed about two thousand pounds and was attached to the hillside with fourteen steel anchors that went several feet into the ground. Many of Kanab's residents were delighted to welcome their old hometown landmark back, and some sent letters of congratulations into the local newspaper, the *Southern Utah News*. Several weeks later, the new wooden K was scattered into pieces by an unusually strong windstorm.

The K in Kanab, Utah, was rebuilt in 2006 after over a year of controversy. —PHOTO BY JIM CORNING

Brett was not about to give up on his project; he sent a brief e-mail to the local paper that read, "The K will return." However, for one new resident to Kanab the idea of having the K on the hillside was more than he could tolerate. He wrote a letter to the newspaper calling the monogram an eyesore and filed complaints with the Bureau of Land Management in both Kanab and Salt Lake City. Shortly afterwards Brett and his father went back to K Hill to clean up the area and consider how to redesign the K. They were met by a local BLM official who informed them that the K could not be replaced because of the complaints that had been filed by a local resident.

For the next six months the controversy over whether or not Kanab should replace its hillside K grew. Everyone had an opinion, and newspapers—even some out-of-town papers—reported on the controversy. While opinions were flying, Brett and his supporters quietly continued to take the necessary steps towards their goal of building a new, more durable K. Eventually, with help from city officials and BLM officials and financial donations from the community, the young scout's dream to rebuild the K became a reality.

On the morning of May 26, 2006, with a signed permit from the BLM on hand and nearly two hundred volunteers to assist, the cement truck began pumping concrete for the K. Because the hillside was so steep, the cement truck wasn't able to get close enough to pump the concrete into the 30-foot-long wooden forms that outlined the K. So the Kanab High School football team formed a bucket brigade to transport the concrete. The boys on the football team were excited to find out which of them would get to pour in the first bucket of concrete, but their coach, Bucky Orton, gave the honor of pouring the first bucket to Brett. After over a year of effort and controversy, Brett's promise to the community that "the K will return" was kept.

K KELSO HIGH SCHOOL
Kelso, Washington

Kelso, Washington, is located along the Cowlitz River in the southwestern corner of the state. Kelso's founder, a Scottish surveyor by the name of Peter Crawford, named it after his hometown in Scotland. The community has always been mindful of its roots, and each September it celebrates its heritage with the Highlander Festival, a weekend of Scottish and Celtic events. Even the high school students pay tribute to their hometown origins by calling themselves the Kelso High Hilanders.

The students at the high school built a wooden K sometime during the 1950s. Through the years the old K had weathered numerous attacks by rivals, and even withstood the 1980 volcanic eruption of Mount St. Helens, only about thirty miles away.

In 1986 the aging K was in need of a major face-lift. Two teachers from Kelso High School, cross-country coach Joe Stewart and woodshop teacher

The community of Kelso, Washington, and its yellow K seen from the air. Even today some historians mistakenly believe hillside letters were built to assist pilots in identifying communities from the air.
—PHOTO BY JOE A. MOILANEN, MOITEK AERIAL IMAGING

Rob Johanson, started making plans to rebuild the old monogram. Then Rick Roberts, a local radio advertising executive, got involved. Roberts drummed up much-needed community support, and within no time the reconstruction of Kelso's K began. For the next six weeks, the cross-country team, teachers, and townspeople contributed expertise, labor, and materials. By October, the volunteers had dismantled the old wooden K and built a new concrete K, complete with a coat of yellow paint.

The K in Kelso is one of only a handful of letters in Washington. Through the years, this high school letter has become a community emblem. The K can best be seen along Interstate 5 or from the air.

	NAME	LOCATION	NOTE
K	Kamiah	Kamiah, ID	A community letter, usually repainted by various school clubs or classes.
K	Kanab	Kanab, UT	Featured on page 81.
KS	Kansas State University	Manhattan, KS	The first K was built in 1915 but fell apart. In 1921, engineering students, accompanied by a brass band and other students of what was then Kansas State Agricultural College—numbering nearly a thousand—marched to Prospect Point to rebuild the concrete K; nine years later the students added the S. Today the KS is a historical landmark maintained by the campus chapter of Tau Beta Pi, an engineering honor society.
K	Kayenta	Kayenta, AZ	A community letter painted white on red sandstone.
K	Kelseyville	Kelseyville, CA	Represents both the community and Kelseyville High School; maintained by the students.
K	Kelso High School	Kelso, WA	Featured on page 83.
K	Kendrick High School	Kendrick, ID	Made of wood.
KF	Kettle Falls	Kettle Falls, WA	Maintained by the community.
K	Kingman High School	Kingman, AZ	Cared for by the student council.
K	Klamath Union High School	Klamath Falls, OR	The students paint their hillside K white three times a year, not only to keep it looking good, but also because their rivals paint it blue or orange.
K	Klein	Klein, MT	The concrete K is maintained by the community since the high school closed.
K	Klickitat	Klickitat, WA	A community letter currently maintained.
KG	Kremlin-Gildford High School	Gildford, MT	The KG was maintained by the students until the school closed in 2005. The letters are no longer cared for but are still visible.

L LA GRANDE HIGH SCHOOL
La Grande, Oregon

Many giant hillside letters have been lost to neglect over time. Such is the case with the L on Table Mountain, overlooking the community of La Grande, Oregon, on the southwest part of town. Although it is now barely visible, a few remains of the rock L can still be seen on the steep incline of this historic mountain, which holds a segment of the old Oregon Trail.

The Oregon Trail was the highway through the West between 1843 and 1869. During this time nearly half a million people used this trail, and one out of ten people died along the way. The pioneers encountered perhaps one of the most difficult parts of the trail as they ascended the steep slopes of Table Mountain with their heavy wagons. Even though this section of the trail was only about a mile and a half long, it took the early pioneers an entire day to travel it.

The L was built just to the north of the old trail over fifty years ago. It was made of rocks and railroad ties, and in the early years the students of La Grande High School would light the L using cans filled with fuel, which they had carried up the hill and placed around the letter. On occasion through the years, rival schools temporarily transformed the L into other letters, and even words. The L was typically white but was sometimes painted other colors for school events.

Photo (c. 1980) of the L in La Grande, Oregon, on the face of Table Mountain, one of the most difficult sections of the historic Oregon Trail. The L is barely visible, but the wagon wheel ruts left by early pioneers can easily be seen. —PHOTO BY JAMES J. PARSONS; COURTESY OF PAUL F. STARRS, UNIVERSITY OF NEVADA–RENO

No one has taken care of the old emblem for years. In addition to remnants of the letter, the wagon wheel ruts left by emigrants on the Oregon Trail over 150 years ago are still visible on the slopes of Table Mountain.

L LAHAINALUNA HIGH SCHOOL
Lahaina, Maui, Hawaii

It may be surprising to many that on a hill overlooking the beautiful island community of Lahaina on Maui is one of the few remaining public boarding schools in the United States, and the oldest school in the United States west of the Rocky Mountains. Reverend Lorrin Andrews opened the school in 1831, and it has been an important educational institution in the community for

175 years. Andrews and his students built the Lahainaluna School as a seminary boarding school for men. Among its first boarders was a gifted native islander by the name of David Malo.

David Malo wrote a book on the ancient beliefs and practices of his people and became a renowned early Hawaiian scholar and philosopher, as well as a Congregational minister. He spent his life in the service of the school and his people. When Malo died in 1853, the students honored him by burying him atop Pu'u Pa'upa'u (Mount Ball), which overlooks his beloved school and community. For over a quarter of a century, Lahainaluna has held an annual celebration called David Malo Day to teach their students the Hawaiian value of giving back to the community, an example Malo had practiced throughout his life.

The L overlooking Lahaina on Maui is nearly eighty years old and is the only known hillside letter in the Hawaiian Islands.
—PHOTO BY JON SHAGAKI, LAHAINALUNA HIGH SCHOOL

Over the years the school has changed hands and names. In 1923, the school became incorporated into the public school system, providing a high school education for the male "boarder students," those who lived in campus dormitories and worked at the school, and "day students," boys and girls from the community who lived at home. (Not until the 1980-1981 school year did female boarders begin attending Lahainaluna.)

In 1929, almost a hundred years after the school first opened, a group of boarder students from what is now Lahainaluna High School cut out the letter L just below the stone-covered grave of David Malo. On their return to campus, they looked back only to see that their crude L was crooked. The following Sunday they hiked back up the steep hillside to straighten it. The small letter they formed remained unchanged for several years. Later the students enlarged the L so it could be seen more clearly, and by the early 1940s they began adding lime to make their letter even more visible.

In 1945, the athletes at Lahainaluna High School set a new Maui Interscholastic League record by winning championships in football, basketball, baseball, and track. To celebrate, the students made four large horizontal bars—one for each championship—inside the L and covered them with powdered lime. Thus a new tradition began. A few years later, in 1954, the students began lighting their L during homecoming and for graduation.

The maintenance of the hillside L over Lahaina continues to be an important school tradition. Each fall and spring students make their way up Pu'u Pa'upa'u to clean and lime their letter, and to pay tribute to David Malo by praying and singing at his gravesite. Just before graduation each year, the seniors prepare five hundred soda cans cut in half and stuffed with rags, and twenty-five torches to light the L, any championship bars, and the last two numbers of their graduating year.

On the night of graduation a group of Lahainaluna alumni wait on Pu'u Pa'upa'u, armed with the torches to light the soda cans, which the seniors had earlier placed around the emblem and filled with diesel fuel. Down below, a special torch, which symbolizes the torch of "learning that cannot be extinguished," is lighted on the graduation stage, signaling to the alumni on Pu'u Pa'upa'u to light the L. As the emblem lights up the night sky, the voices of the senior boarder students fill the air with "Yonder Lahaina Mountains," a song describing the beauty of their island and the school they love.

In 2006 the school celebrated its 175th anniversary, with over three thousand people attending a pageant and festivities. If you visit Maui, it might be tempting to hike to the letter overlooking Lahainaluna High School; however, because it is on private land the school asks that you admire the L from afar.

LP LONE PINE
Lone Pine, California

A whitewashed rock LP stands out against the Alabama Hills to the west of Lone Pine, a town in the Owens Valley in east-central California. The exact date and circumstances of the construction of the LP are unknown, but locals believe that the letters have been around since the 1930s.

Lone Pine was named for a single pine tree that grew at the mouth of Lone Pine Canyon. It is a place of exceptional beauty, with its backdrop of Mount Whitney, the highest peak in the contiguous United States. Just outside of Lone Pine are the remains of the Manzanar relocation camp for Japanese Americans during World War II.

In 1943 and 1944 Ansel Adams came to Lone Pine to photograph the camp and its detainees. On one of his visits, Adams captured his famous photograph "Winter Sunrise, Sierra Nevada from Lone Pine, California." Apparently, however, Adams did not appreciate the distinctive hometown flavor added by the hillside LP, and he brushed out the intruding letters from his negative. When it was later discovered what Adams had done, he was criticized for not being

Ansel Adams removed the LP, which stands for Lone Pine, from his famous photo "Winter Sunrise, Sierra Nevada from Lone Pine, California." James J. Parsons took this photo resembling Adams's famous one, but with the LP intact. —PHOTO BY JAMES J. PARSONS; COURTESY OF PAUL F. STARRS, UNIVERSITY OF NEVADA–RENO

true to the reality of his subject. To this Adams later explained that he wasn't about to perpetuate the scar and destroy the perfection of the scene.

Adams was not the only one who tried to get rid of the LP. In about 1995 a government official representing the Bureau of Land Management tried to have the LP removed from the hillside. The town council and community immediately protested. There was such an outcry that the BLM retreated and let the community keep its emblem. The students at the high school maintain the letter, and local businesses lend their support by donating paint and equipment. Despite occasional opposition, the LP remains a hometown landmark of Lone Pine.

LMU LOYOLA MARYMOUNT UNIVERSITY
Los Angeles, California

Loyola Marymount University had its beginnings in 1865 as St. Vincent's College, a Catholic school for men, and it became one of the most prominent men's schools in the state. In 1929 the newly built Loyola College of Los Angeles hired a construction company to build an L on the bluff near the school. The young men of Loyola took great pride in their new hillside letter. The following year Loyola was granted university status and became Loyola University of Los Angeles.

Near the Loyola campus in 1923, the Religious of the Sacred Heart of Mary opened a school for women, which later joined St. Joseph College of Orange, a four-year liberal arts college for women, and eventually became Marymount College of Orange. In 1970 Loyola University merged with Marymount College, forming Loyola Marymount University.

The LMU Bluff is a well-known landmark in Los Angeles. —GLENN CRATTY, LOYOLA MARYMOUNT UNIVERSITY

After nearly a hundred years of being an all-male school, the idea of sharing their campus with women didn't settle well with some of the male students. The ladies soon had enough of the Loyola men's attitude, so they devised a plan. Shortly after the merger, under the cover of darkness, the ladies changed the men's L to a periwinkle blue M, their former school color and letter.

The women's daring action took the young men by surprise and eventually helped unite them as a university. In 1973 the letters M and U were added to the L in recognition of the official merger of the two great institutions. Today the LMU for Loyola Marymount University is a well-known landmark in Los Angeles.

	NAME	LOCATION	NOTE
L	La Grande High School	La Grande, OR	Featured on page 86.
L	La Madera	La Madera, NM	Visible along U.S. 285.
L	La Salle High School	Union Gap, WA	Built by a senior class as a gift to the school.
L	La Verkin	La Verkin, UT	A rock letter maintained by the community.
LA	Laguna-Acoma High School	New Laguna, NM	Maintained by the students.
L	Lahainaluna High School	Lahaina, Maui, HI	Featured on page 87.
L	Lassen County High School	Susanville, CA	Maintained occasionally by the senior class.
L	Lava Hot Springs	Lava Hot Springs, ID	A community letter cared for by the townsfolk.
L	Lavina High School	Lavina, MT	Maintained by the students.
L	Laytonville	Laytonville, CA	Maintained by the community.
LV	Lee Vining High School	Lee Vining, CA	Maintained by the students.
L	Leeds	Leeds, UT	A community letter maintained by the townspeople.
L	Lewiston	Lewiston, ID	The L represents both Lewiston High School and the community and is maintained by both groups.

	NAME	LOCATION	NOTE
L	Lewistown	Lewistown, MT	Dismantled during the 1980s because of vandalism.
L	Libby	Libby, MT	Maintained by the alumni of Libby High School.
L	Lincoln County High School	Eureka, MT	The whitewashed rock L is painted by the senior class for homecoming.
L	Lincoln County High School	Panaca, NV	The L was built in 1927.
LP	Lone Pine	Lone Pine, CA	Featured on page 90.
L	Lordsburg	Lordsburg, NM	Located on a small butte just west of town, the L is no longer maintained and is barely visible.
LA	Los Alamos High School	Los Alamos, NM	During the 1960s some scientists working with the Atomic Energy Commission felt the letters were unsightly, and they were removed. This led to a hearing, which resulted in the federal government rebuilding the school's letters. The LA is maintained by the seniors.
LL	Los Lunas	Los Lunas, NM	A school and community emblem maintained by the students of Los Lunas High School.
L	Lovell	Lovell, WY	Visible but presently not maintained.
L	Lovelock	Lovelock, NV	Built in 1931, the letter is visible and maintained by community organizations.
L	Loyalton	Loyalton, CA	Represents the community; maintained by the students of Loyalton High School.
LMU	Loyola Marymount University	Los Angeles, CA	Featured on page 92.
L	Loyola Sacred Heart High School	Missoula, MT	The L on Mount Jumbo represents the school and has been maintained by Loyola students since it was built of rocks in 1961. The school filled the L with concrete in 2001 to stop frequent rearranging of the rocks. See story and photo on pages 15–16.
L	Ludlow	Ludlow, CA	A rock L overlooks the town of Ludlow, once a bustling mining community of nearly two thousand residents. With its current population of twenty-five, Ludlow is now considered a ghost town.
L	Lyons	Lyons, CO	Represents Lyons Middle-Senior High School and the community; the senior class paints the rock L each year and adds their class year below it.

M MINERS OF THE COLORADO SCHOOL OF MINES
Golden, Colorado

During the second half of the nineteenth century, central Colorado was teeming with miners looking for gold. In 1866 the Reverend George M. Randall made plans for a university west of Denver in Golden, Colorado, which would later become the Colorado School of Mines.

In 1905, the same year that students at Berkeley built the first hillside letter, senior Joseph O'Byrne was asked to design a hillside M—for "Miners," as the students were called—as an assignment in his descriptive geometry class. The task entailed mathematically designing a letter that would appear undistorted from any angle. The letter was to be constructed west of Golden on the rocky twenty-three-degree slope of Mount Zion, at an elevation of 6,900 feet. Joe's detailed drawing turned out to be perfect. However, it was three years before the school constructed the M designed by O'Byrne. When the Miners' monogram was finally built, it took only one afternoon, 250 students, twenty teachers, and a supply train of burros to complete the 104-by-107-foot rock M. It was the fourth hillside letter in the nation and the first in the state of Colorado.

The Miners have always loved their M, and through the years they have been fearless in protecting it from rival schools. In 1919, right before the big football game of the season with their archrival, the University of Denver, a

The M for the Miners of the Colorado School of Mines in Golden was the fourth hillside letter built in the nation. —COURTESY OF THE COLORADO SCHOOL OF MINES ALUMNI ASSOCIATION

taxi-load of students from Denver arrived in town to paint the M gold and crimson, Denver's school colors.

The Miners discovered their intentions, and with Wild West drama they barricaded the road and stopped the taxi at gunpoint. The newspapers reported that gunfire was exchanged but no one was hurt. However, the University of Denver students were taken prisoner, given workman's coveralls, and had their heads shaved. As a final insult the Miners painted the letter M on the foreheads of the Denver students using silver nitrate (which remains for about six months), as a warning to any other Denver students who might be thinking of trying to claim jump the Miner's much-loved M.

The M on Mount Zion overlooks the Colorado School of Mines and Golden at an elevation of 6,900 feet. —PHOTO BY JAMES J. PARSONS; COURTESY OF PAUL F. STARRS, UNIVERSITY OF NEVADA–RENO

In more recent years, a tradition called the M Climb takes place right before fall classes begin. Each member of the freshman class carries up a rock of ten pounds or so to place on the M, as a symbol of his or her career as a student at the school. Besides being a lot of fun, this activity encourages incoming freshmen to get involved in the traditions of the university. The freshmen bring rocks from all over the country; many students select a special rock from home just for this purpose. On the day of the climb, food stands dot the trail to the M, providing drinks and other refreshments for the students. Fraternity and sorority students are stationed along the way to make sure the freshmen's rocks measure up. At the M, upperclassmen are waiting to help whitewash the new rocks and the occasional unsuspecting freshman.

In the spring the graduating seniors trek to the top of Mount Zion to white-wash the M as their departing tribute to the school. Many remove the rock they placed there as a freshman and keep it as a personal memento of their time at the Colorado School of Mines.

For homecoming in 1931, the Miners' M became the first landmark letter to be lighted using electricity. The following year the M was again lighted, and it has shone brightly every night since (see photo on page 13). Even when the lights have to be repaired, the Miners keep the M shining with extra lights and a generator or two. Today the lights change color for holidays and special occasions, thanks to the hard work and financial support of the Blue Key, a national leadership and service fraternity, and the students.

 ## MINERS OF MONTANA TECH
Butte, Montana

The M in Butte, representing the Miners (students) of what is now Montana Tech of the University of Montana, has the distinction of being Montana's only hillside letter that is lighted throughout the year. In 1910, there were only about fifty students enrolled at the Montana State School of Mines. This handful of students designed, surveyed, and built the second hillside M in Montana. No one knows what inspired them, but sometime in March of 1910, three soon-to-be-graduating seniors, August Grunert, Walter H. Jensen, and William Stuewe Jr., surveyed and laid out a giant M on Big Butte.

During the next two weeks, some thirty-five other students and teachers hauled and placed an estimated 441 tons of rhyolite (a type of volcanic rock) in the 75-foot-wide by 91-foot-long outline of the M. On the school's first official "M Day," all fifty students and their teachers hauled water and lime up the steep hillside to give their M its first whitewashing. This became one of the school's longest-lasting traditions. Two years later serifs were added to the letter, making it 90 feet wide.

The M overlooking Butte, Montana, has shone brightly each night since 1962. The city celebrates the Fourth of July with fireworks over the M. —PHOTO BY LISA HORNSTEIN-KUNKEL

In 1962 the governor of Montana, Tim Babcock, made a visit to Butte's M and was given the honor of turning on its new electric lights. The governor remarked that night that the M in Butte symbolized "what can be done where the spirit of cooperation is present." How right he was. Nearly a century after it was built, the rock M overlooking Butte is still lighting up Montana's big sky each and every night.

M MINERS OF NEW MEXICO TECH
Socorro, New Mexico

The rock M west of Socorro in central New Mexico was built at an elevation of over 7,200 feet on Socorro Peak. The M was built to represent the New Mexico School of Mines, which is now the New Mexico Institute of Mining and Technology (or New Mexico Tech). The early Miners, as the students are called, selected a peak that is difficult to reach. Because of its location the M has never been attacked by rival schools, and over the years it has proved quite a challenge to students who have maintained it.

The origin of the M has been "sadly lost in the mist of time," writes Robert Eveleth, history buff of the M and senior mining engineer for the New Mexico Bureau of Mines and Mineral Resources at New Mexico Tech. Eveleth estimates the beginning of the M sometime between the years 1911 and 1912. He bases this conclusion on a number of sources, including the notes written by J. Avery Smith, a member of the class of 1913, who wrote that he "provided two burros for the first load of lime and water," and also commented that the M was laid out using a "Brunton compass and steel tape." Another source was the survey notebook of Frank "Instrument Man" Maloit. It was Maloit who first surveyed the M on Socorro Peak. However, the original idea for a Miner's M belonged to Horace Lyons, also a member of the class of 1913.

In the beginning, maintenance of the M was an unorganized affair, but by about 1919 a two-day outing that included an overnight campout was formally set aside each year for whitewashing. The sophomores and freshmen were assigned the duty. The students carried heavy sacks of lime on their backs up the steep mountainside. Since there was no water at the top, the students often waited until the first snowfall, letting Mother Nature provide the water to mix in with the lime.

As time went on, the tradition of carrying sacks of lime up Socorro Peak has turned into the annual M Mountain Run, a contest open to anyone. Each person carries a fifty-pound sack of marble quartz (the substitute for lime) while they race up the steep, rocky, cactus-strewn mountainside. The first five people to accomplish this feat get fifty dollars and a T-shirt, and all participants are treated to lunch.

The M on Socorro Peak also has the distinction of being the first tee for the Elfego Baca Golf Shoot, which *The Book of Lists* calls "one of the world's

The M on Socorro Peak west of Socorro, New Mexico, is the first tee for the Elfego Baca Golf Shoot.
—PHOTO BY GEORGE ZAMORA, NEW MEXICO INSTITUTE OF MINING AND TECHNOLOGY

most unusual golf events." Each golfer brings three spotters, old clubs, and a lot of luck. The participants tee off near the M, from a wooden platform at an elevation of 7,243 feet. The golfers start with ten balls, and the one who ends the shoot with the fewest number of shots and at least one ball wins. The final hole is a fifty-foot patch of dirt on the New Mexico Tech campus almost three miles away and 2,550 feet down.

The M now has electric lights and is lighted during the first week of school, finals week, 49ers' Days (homecoming), and other designated special occasions. The Miners of New Mexico Tech share their M with the Warriors of Socorro High School; the M becomes a lighted W whenever the high school has an important game or other event.

M MINERS OF THE UNIVERSITY OF TEXAS–EL PASO
El Paso, Texas

In 1913 the Texas State School of Mines and Metallurgy opened its doors in El Paso, Texas. Ten years later, the students of the school, by that time called Texas College of Mines (TCM), built and painted a white rock M on the Franklin Mountains, where it remained until the early 1960s. In 1966, the M was moved to its current location overlooking the football stadium, the Sun Bowl. The building of the new M coincided with the school's name change to Texas Western College of the University of Texas at El Paso, which was shortened to the University of Texas at El Paso, or UTEP.

Every March since the 1920s, the engineering and mining students have celebrated TCM Day by painting green shamrocks all over campus and on themselves, and painting their hillside M white. TCM Day, the oldest tradition on campus, not only honors the patron saint of engineering, St. Patrick, but also remembers the roots of the university—mining and metallurgy. During the 1920s students were blindfolded and asked to kiss the Blarney Stone, which had been doused with green paint, and then they paid homage to St. Patrick by participating in planned activities of the day. Those that complied were given a "Green Card," along with a picnic lunch.

TCM Day was always an upbeat celebration until 1948, when the engineering students along with geology and chemistry students protested the addition of a liberal arts college to their campus. To show their opposition, the engineering students divided the campus into an east and west section using, of course, green paint. The west side was Texas College of Mines, and the east side Texas Western College.

Today the mining, geology, and metallurgy students still carry on the Miners' TCM Day traditions of painting the M, painting shamrocks throughout campus, and kissing the Blarney Stone. They also do community service, clean

The giant rock M located above
the Sun Bowl of the University of
Texas–El Paso. —COURTESY OF THE
UNIVERSITY OF TEXAS– EL PASO/UNIVERSITY
COMMUNICATIONS

Students of UTEP paint their M
in honor of St. Patrick, the patron
saint of engineering. —COURTESY
OF THE UNIVERSITY OF TEXAS–EL PASO/
UNIVERSITY COMMUNICATIONS

parts of the university grounds, parade through campus singing the engineering fight song, and symbolically reclaim the campus by painting green lines on the grounds and raising the Texas College of Mines flag in the center of campus, all in honor of those early Miners who staked out the first M on the Franklin Mountains.

M MONTANA STATE UNIVERSITY
Bozeman, Montana

The M belonging to Montana State University in Bozeman is located on the southwest slope of Mount Baldy, about five miles northeast of campus. The letter resulted from a custom that each class leaves a memorial, or gift, to the school. The class of 1918 chose to build a hillside letter as its gift. When the 100-foot-wide, 240-foot-long M was built for what was then Montana State College, the students heralded their new letter as the largest, a claim often made by enthusiastic letter builders. (At that point Brigham Young University's Y was still the largest.)

Bozeman's M was first laid out by the school's civil engineering students, with Albert Borton and David "Sloppy" Thomas doing much of the surveying work. Before any construction could begin, however, the school first had to secure a permit from the Gallatin National Forest. Borton and classmate Thomas Ross met with Ralph E. Bodley, the supervisor of the Gallatin National Forest, and presented their request to build a permanent landmark on national forest land. They must have been persuasive young men because Bodley granted the first-ever permit of this kind to the school.

The M was built on October 24, 1915. Construction began at four thirty in the morning. It was cold and dark when the men of the class of 1918 made their way to the base of Mount Baldy by way of bicycles, buggies, and one truck to begin building the M. It took the men all day to collect and dislodge enough rock to fill in the surveyed letter. Sometimes the rock they loosened would bounce down the hill a hundred feet or more. While the men worked on the hill, the women of the class of 1918 fixed and served them a picnic-style lunch. The rock M was basically finished by sunset, with a few final touches added some nine months later.

Marsha Johnson Haynes, a member of the class of 1918, said years later, "The M was erected as a lasting monument to the spirit and industry of the class of 1918, but principally as a mark of their devotion to Montana State College." Through the years, thousands of students have helped maintain the M on Mount Baldy, continuing the tradition begun by the class of 1918.

The hillside M of Montana State University in Bozeman, five miles from campus on Mount Baldy, was built in 1915. —COURTESY OF MONTANA STATE UNIVERSITY

MSAC MOUNT SAN ANTONIO COLLEGE
Walnut, California

The hillside letters MSAC in Walnut, California, stand for Mount San Antonio College. The MSAC is unique among college emblems. Not only is it the only school emblem with four letters, but it is the only double emblem: there is an MSAC on two hills, one on the south and one on the north side of campus.

The first letters to appear were an SA on the south hill, called SA Hill, built by students and a college maintenance crew. As the story goes, the letters were built as a landmark so that visitors could find their way around the campus after dark. A maintenance man used a bulldozer to cut a road up the back side of the hill and scrape off the cactus and bushes from the letter site on the south slope. Following this, Barney Conrad's surveying class laid out the letters with stakes and string. The maintenance crew followed, hauling in thousands of broken pieces of concrete from old floors of demolished campus buildings to fill in the formed outline of the letters. Wet concrete was added to the forms to complete the job, just in time for the school's first night football game in 1948.

Mount San Antonio College has two identical MSACs on hillsides to the north and south of campus. —MT. SAN ANTONIO COLLEGE PHOTO

106

After the last football game of the season, the maintenance crew headed up the hill again to spray-paint the letter with white traffic paint. Later the letters M and C were added, and sometime during the late fifties the school added a second MSAC to the hill on the north side of campus, called Monogram Hill.

Most schools have unique traditions associated with the maintenance and painting of their hillside emblem. Mount San Antonio College is no exception. Beginning in the late 1950s, the freshmen were required to scrub the school's multiple-lettered emblem using toothbrushes while the sophomores supervised. Today many MSAC freshmen are grateful that this tradition is no longer practiced.

M THE UNIVERSITY OF MONTANA
Missoula, Montana

The University of Montana's M in Missoula is the oldest landmark letter in the state. In 1909 the junior class built the school's first M, a small, white-washed rock letter that was located just below the site of the present M on Mount Sentinel at the eastern edge of the campus.

In the spring of 1912 the sophomore class built a wooden M that stood upright. This new and improved M cost the students eighteen dollars and included lights, to be used only for special occasions. Then in September of that year the sophomores turned over care and maintenance of the upright M to the freshman class, resulting in a tradition that continues today.

In 1913 a much larger M was constructed of wood, but it did not last long; the sophomores transformed the letter into the number 14, their graduating year. The large wooden 14 was remade into an M, but then Mother Nature came along and destroyed it in a blizzard, leaving only a pile of wood at the foot of the hill.

The 100-by-125-foot M in Missoula, Montana, is a very popular hiking destination. The M trail, with its thirteen switchbacks, climbs 600 feet to a stunning view of the valley below. —COURTESY OF THE UNIVERSITY OF MONTANA

In the fall of 1915, assistant professor of forestry James H. Bonner and members of his surveying class selected and surveyed the present site of the M on Mount Sentinel. Once this was done, a long line of students positioned themselves side by side up the steep hill to relay by bucket brigade thousands of pounds of shale, which they used to outline the M. Then they filled in the outline with granite rocks and gave it a heavy coat of whitewash. The following spring, the freshman class completed some final details. The new M measured 100 by 60 feet.

Caring for the new M continued to be a compulsory assignment for all freshmen. However, during the 1960s, school spirit dwindled and the university decided to replace the fifty-three-year-old rock emblem with a concrete M, which would require less maintenance. In 1968 the university spent $4,328 to build the new 100-foot-wide, 125-foot-long M.

Through the years the M in Missoula, like many other hillside letters, has on occasion been lighted. Beginning in 1912, the sophomore class purchased lights for their wooden upright M. When that M was destroyed in 1914, so were the lights. Then in 1919 the freshman men, after completing the annual whitewashing, decided to illuminate the M in red using fuses from the local railroad station. This proved to be so popular that the lighting of the M has become a homecoming tradition.

Mount Sentinel and the M provide a handsome backdrop to the University of Montana campus. The trail to the M, zigzagging 600 feet up the hill, is a favorite recreational site for students and other residents, as well as tourists. In fact, "doin' the M" is a common workout activity for Missoulians. Thousands of people of all ages walk, run, or jog to the M each year; it has become a part of the culture of Missoula. The M is cared for annually by student organizations under the direction of the university's facilities services. Local businesses donate the paint and students provide the labor, ensuring that one of Missoula's favorite landmarks is always looking its best.

M THE UNIVERSITY OF MONTANA–WESTERN
Dillon, Montana

The University of Montana–Western in Dillon opened in 1893 as the Montana State Normal School. Two years later it became Montana State Normal College. When the fifty members of the class of 1919 graduated from the college, they contributed $400 to their school, the equivalent of about $4,000 today. Rather than designating the gift for laboratory equipment, books, or even scholarships, the class of 1919 wanted the college to have a hillside emblem.

Three other postsecondary schools in Montana each had a giant M. Montana State University in Bozeman had just built one a year earlier. With this in mind, the seniors of 1919 selected a spot for their letter on a prominent nearby hillside to the west of campus. However, the actual work didn't begin until the following year.

In 1920 Professor Wiseman, who taught manual training (woodworking and other practical arts), drew a simple line design of the M and staked its outline in the area designated by the class of 1919. The male students of the normal college filled in the outlined area with stones and whitewashed the letter. When the job was done, the school had an M measuring 120 feet each way, at a cost of $100, with $300 left for maintenance of the letter.

In 1925 the male students of the college formed the M Club, which consisted of anyone who lettered in athletics while attending the school. In the beginning,

The M in Dillon, built in 1920, represents the University of Montana–Western. It was the last M built of the four Ms belonging to the Montana University System. —PHOTO BY WALLY FELDT

only men participated in athletics, so it was an all-male club until the 1960s. The M Club took on the responsibility of painting and maintaining the M every year on M Day while other students raked and cleaned up the campus.

During the ensuing years, the school changed names four more times, and there were changes for the M as well. In May 1941, the men of M Club thought they should give their school emblem a double coat of paint, knowing that most of them would be called to serve in World War II and might not be back. Instead, the young men decided to paint it red, white, and blue as their final patriotic gesture before they left for the war.

In 1954, rival students of Montana Tech dynamited the M, and in 1995 the M Club disbanded and the M was left to the elements of nature. Today it is uncertain just who is looking after the University of Montana–Western's hillside letter. Although it is still visible, it is not well maintained. As of 2006, a group of alumni, including some former members of the M Club, are looking into refurbishing Western's M.

	NAME	LOCATION	NOTE
M	Madras	Madras, OR	It is uncertain who maintains the M, but it is still visible.
M	Magdalena	Magdalena, NM	The seniors of Magdalena High School maintain the community's rock M annually.
M	Malad	Malad City, ID	Painted by the seniors or student council of the Malad Senior High School. On occasion the community lights the M for the Fourth of July or for the high school homecoming.
M	Malta	Malta, MT	The community's first M was removed years ago. In 2004 the senior class of Malta High School built another M, about seven miles from town along U.S. 2.
M	Manassa	Manassa, CO	The small town of Manassa has had a rock M on its hillside since 1959, when the community was large enough to support a high school. Now community groups keep the M looking its best.

	NAME	LOCATION	NOTE
M	Manti High School	Manti, UT	The student government oversees the maintenance of the M; they whitewash it each year and light it unless fire danger exists due to dry weather conditions.
M	Mapleton High School	Mapleton, OR	Located above the high school football field; maintained by the M Club, a student athletic group.
M	Marathon	Marathon, TX	No longer maintained and fading from view.
M	Maricopa	Maricopa, CA	Represents both Maricopa High School and the community; maintained annually by the Big M Club, a boys' sports club at the school.
M	Maricopa High School	Maricopa, AZ	The M on Pima Butte was built and painted in 1955 by the first graduating class. The teachers and students measured the outline, then carried rocks, water, lime, and brooms up the hill to build their emblem, which is still maintained by the students.
M	Marist College	Poughkeepsie, NY	The M for Marist College, one of a handful of hillside letters east of the Rocky Mountains, is a red and white letter painted by the school's rowing team on a natural rock wall along the west side of the Hudson River.
M	Marysvale	Marysvale, UT	Outlined in rock and maintained by community and youth groups.
M	Mayer Junior-Senior High School	Mayer, AZ	Painted by the football team each year.
M	Mazama High School	Klamath Falls, OR	Each year on Paint the M Day, students climb up to the rock M and whitewash it.
M	McCamey	McCamey, TX	A painted white community letter, the M is lighted by the townsfolk for the high school homecoming game.
M	McLoughlin High School	Milton-Freewater, OR	The leadership class at "Mac-Hi" maintains the M, which was previously a painted letter but is now made of wood and painted red.
M	Meeteetse High School	Meeteetse, WY	The Meeteetse High School Longhorns added longhorns to their rock M, which they maintain. See photo on page 3.
MV	Mesa Vista High School	Ojo Caliente, NM	The rock MV is painted by the seniors, but on their own time.
M	Miami High School	Miami, AZ	Cared for by the students, who often have to paint it more than once a year because their rivals from Globe like to paint it black.
M	Milford High School	Milford, UT	Removed.
M	Miners of the Colorado School of Mines	Golden, CO	Featured on page 95. See also photo on page 13.
M	Miners of Montana Tech	Butte, MT	Featured on page 98.
M	Miners of New Mexico Tech	Socorro, NM	Featured on page 99.

	NAME	LOCATION	NOTE
M	Miners of the University of Texas–El Paso	El Paso, TX	Featured on page 102.
M	Miners of the University of Wisconsin–Platteville	Platteville, WI	The M on Platte Mound was built to honor the Miners (students) of the Engineering Department of Wisconsin State University, now the University of Wisconsin–Platteville. It began when a group of spirited hikers formed an M in two feet of snow back in the winter of 1936. In 1937 a large group of underclassmen, supervised by seniors, used hand picks, crowbars, and wheelbarrows to build a gigantic M measuring 214 feet wide by 241 feet long; they claimed it was the "Biggest M in the World." It is still maintained by the students.
M	Mission College Preparatory Catholic High School	San Luis Obispo, CA	First built by the Mission Central Catholic School, which closed in 1970 and reopened in 1983 as the Mission College Preparatory Catholic High School. The letter is maintained by the freshman class.
M	Moapa Valley High School	Overton, NV	The M was built in 1930 by the students.
M	Monrovia	Monrovia, CA	Represents the community and is maintained by the townspeople, who support Monrovia High School by lighting the M during a game. If Monrovia High wins, the M becomes a V to announce the victory. The letter is also lighted the night of high school graduation.
M	Montana State University	Bozeman, MT	Featured on page 104.
M	Montpelier	Montpelier, ID	The M was built in 1923 and is still maintained.
M	Morenci	Morenci, AZ	No longer maintained and fading from view.
MV	Moreno Valley	Moreno Valley, CA	Cared for by community groups.
M	Moroni	Moroni, UT	Removed.
MB	Morro Bay	Morro Bay, CA	The MB represents both Morro Bay High School and the community. The letters are usually blue and white, the school colors, except when Morro Bay's rivals from Coast Union High School in Cambria paint them yellow and red.
MSAC	Mount San Antonio College	Walnut, CA	Featured on page 106.
MC	Mountain Crest High School	Hyrum, UT	Maintained by the students.
M	The University of Montana	Missoula, MT	Featured on page 107.
M	The University of Montana–Western	Dillon, MT	Featured on page 109.

N UNIVERSITY OF NEVADA–RENO
Reno, Nevada

Clarke Webster and Harvey McPhail, juniors at the University of Nevada in 1913, didn't like the place their surveying class had chosen for Nevada's first hillside letter. So the two continued looking. They found a location they both liked east of campus on Peavine Peak, overlooking the Truckee Meadows and the city of Reno. Years ago these meadows, and the Truckee River flowing through them, were a favorite resting place for many tired pioneers and their hungry animals traveling west. Webster and McPhail used a transit (a portable instrument for surveying), stakes, and some string, to lay out a gigantic letter N for the University of Nevada.

The outlined N measured 140 feet wide and 150 feet in length. The following Sunday, March 13, 1913, other students joined in to help. Soon the mountainside was filled with enthusiastic students piling rocks within the stringed outline of the letter. Thousands of rocks were placed by hand. Then some of the Nevada boys wanting to take a gamble climbed farther up the slope, and with cries of warning to those below they started rolling several rocks—weighing tons—down the mountain. Lady Luck seems to have been with them, because all but one of the boulders rolled right into the N, and the one that missed the letter continued to roll harmlessly down the mountainside. By late Thursday night the following week, the rock N was finished, including the whitewashing, making it the first of approximately forty-three landmark letters built in Nevada.

The N above the University of Nevada– Reno is the state's oldest hillside letter. —PHOTO BY JEAN DIXON

Two months after the N appeared on Peavine Peak, the student newspaper published a poem entitled "The Big N" in its May 1, 1913, issue:

You'r the child of college pep,
Whose home Nevada claims.
You'r to tell the people coming
Of our hopes, our mighty aims.

You'r to tell of sweaty labor,
Of a ditching party too.
How we toiled and moiled and plotted
To build you strong and true.

How we saw you full completed,
A blazing beacon light.
For the help and inspiration
Of our successors in the fight.

Be proud of your sagebrush jacket,
Your rugged [painted] face.
For Nevada sons hope only,
That you'll warm them from disgrace.

Watch forever, now we charge you,
Make Nevada's sons all men;
Make them keen, and good and stalwart.
We bow to you Big N.

For years the students of the University of Nevada have whitewashed and maintained their hillside letter. However, as time has passed, student interest has dwindled, so the Young Alumni Chapter of the University of Nevada has taken over caring for the N, which is approaching its one-hundredth birthday.

	NAME	LOCATION	NOTE
NS	North Sevier High School	Salina, UT	The NS is no longer maintained by the high school, but on occasion alumni have repainted it.
N	University of Nevada–Reno	Reno, NV	Featured on page 114.

OK OKANOGAN HIGH SCHOOL
Okanogan, Washington

When travelers enter Okanogan, Washington, off Route 20, they are immediately greeted with hillside after hillside of orchards. Fruit is plentiful in this peaceful community that sits along the banks of the Okanogan River, and so is school spirit. The students of Okanogan High School in northern Washington decided they wanted to construct their school's emblem—in this case the letters OK—using plywood. They placed the OK on a hillside directly behind the high school in the west part of town. No one is exactly certain how long this first OK lasted, but most folks say it was around for about ten years.

In 2003 a large grass fire raced across the hillside behind the school. Aaron Nickelson, a history teacher, noticed that the flames were getting very close to the school's hillside emblem. He quickly headed up the hill and began digging a fire trench around the plywood OK. Nickelson's quick thinking saved the school's letters.

In 2005, the Okanogan High School seniors decided that for their class service project they would rebuild and paint the seared and aging OK. After completing the project, the seniors thought it would be nice to have the OK stand upright, like the HOLLYWOOD sign in California. After quite a bit of work, they finally got their emblem to stand and headed down the hill back to school. The seniors had not been back long when an announcement came over the school's loudspeaker that there had been a "big snafu with the Big

The wooden OK in Okanogan, Washington, is a relatively recent addition to the small hillside alphabet of Washington.
—PHOTO BY JIM CORNING

OK." The OK had fallen. The seniors returned to the hill and cleaned off their emblem, leaving it flat on the ground, where it remains today. Even if their hillside letter didn't stand up like HOLLYWOOD, that was OK with them.

OT OREGON TECH
Klamath Falls, Oregon

The community of Klamath Falls in southern Oregon has four separate hillside emblems, one of which is the OT representing the Oregon Institute of Technology, or Oregon Tech. The school's first home was located on the site of a World War II Marine Corps recuperation facility beginning in 1947. The remains of the first O the students built, probably a cutout letter, can still be seen above the old campus during light snowfalls. In 1964 the school relocated

The OT for Oregon Tech was completed in 1981, making it a newcomer among postsecondary school hillside letters. —COURTESY OF OREGON INSTITUTE OF TECHNOLOGY

to its present campus, and the students built a second O on a hillside north of campus sometime between 1964 and 1966. The rock O was whitewashed each year by the freshmen, a project coordinated by the Ioto Phi Theta fraternity until the 1970s, when Phi Delta Theta took over the effort.

Like many emblems made of rocks, the O was transformed into other symbols and words through the years. One morning in spring 1976, the campus awoke to find the Playboy bunny symbol in place of the O. This was more than President Winston Purvine could tolerate, and he ordered that the whitewashed rocks be scattered down the steep hillside. Eventually, after tempers had cooled, students tried and failed to come up with a material less moveable than rocks, such as grass or concrete. But the steepness of the grade made rock the best solution, and the rock O was rebuilt. Then, in 1981, the Phi Delta Theta fraternity added a T to the inside of the O using whitewashed railroad ties and gravel.

Until the early nineties, when the school's football program ended, the students would outline the O with lights as part of their homecoming celebration.

119

In the beginning, the students used lanterns or flares for illumination, until one windy night when a flare tipped over and set the hillside on fire. No people or buildings were harmed, but it did upset a meeting of the president's advisory council.

Today the twenty-five-year-old emblem is still maintained by Phi Delta Theta. The letters still get modified now and then by other campus fraternities, but they are quickly restored as the OT, the landmark letters of Oregon Tech.

O OROVILLE HIGH SCHOOL
Oroville, California

Most high school letters are built by an entire school or class, but not Oroville's O. Just a small group of enthusiastic boys, supportive parents, and a few girls with food saw this project through to the end.

Rusty Jacobs, the 1929 student body president of Oroville High School, said there would be an O on Table Mountain even if he and his friend Morrow Steadman had to build it themselves, and they almost did. The letter O sits on Table Mountain northeast of the community of Oroville—sometimes called the "City of Gold"—about seventy miles north of Sacramento. During the gold rush days of the 1800s, Oroville was one of the largest cities in California.

It is a very strenuous climb to reach the 33-by-87-foot letter, and the high school boys back in 1929 did it carrying sacks of concrete on their backs. The O was actually Morrow Steadman's idea. He was inspired by the Big C at the University of California–Berkeley, which was the first of approximately sixty-three letters built in the state. Getting a small group of boys together, Steadman and his brother, Ernie, began the project. Douglas Chambers had the task of surveying and laying out the letter. Applying all that he had learned in his high school math class, and using a transit (a surveying instrument), Chambers and the other boys took readings from the school and

The Oroville O, built in 1929, was inspired by the University of California–Berkeley's C.
—PHOTO BY JAMES J. PARSONS; COURTESY OF PAUL F. STARRS, UNIVERSITY OF NEVADA–RENO

the mountain. Next, they laid a huge paper O on the mountainside and critiqued the shape of the letter, making necessary adjustments.

After the surveying was completed, this small group of industrious boys built a sled to help them pull drums of water, a gasoline mixer, and other heavy items up the steep terrain. They began gathering basalt (lava) rocks to build the O. Jay Johnson's father, who owned an automobile repair shop, furnished the boys with a supply of old axles to wedge in between the large cracks of rocks before pouring in the concrete. The boys hauled 108 sacks of concrete up Table Mountain.

The work of building the O went slowly, until Ernie invited the high school girls to bring food. After that the pace picked up. Two months later the O was completed, and the builders held a dedication ceremony on June 8, 1929, presenting the letter to the school. Morrow Steadman later wrote that he hoped the O would last through generations and remind students of the importance of cooperation and teamwork, on the athletic field and in school.

Some fifty years later Dan Wilson, a local reporter, printed the story of the O in the *Oroville Mercury Register*. The folks of Oroville were so moved by the hard work and dedication of young Steadman and Jacobs that some folks made financial contributions to ensure the letter's preservation. Today, some efforts are being made to declare this community landmark a state historical site.

	NAME	LOCATION	NOTE
O	Oakley	Oakley, ID	Technically not on a hillside, the O is painted on a nearby earth and rock dam.
OK	Okanogan High School	Okanogan, WA	Featured on page 117.
O	Olympus High School	Salt Lake City, UT	Maintained and lighted during homecoming.
O	Orange Union High School	Orange, CA	The O was built in 1917; the school was replaced by Orange High School, and the letter no longer exists.
OT	Oregon Tech	Klamath Falls, OR	Featured on page 118.
O	Orofino High School	Orofino, ID	Made of tin and painted white with blue trim, this large O overlooks the high school and is maintained by students.
O	Oroville High School	Oroville, CA	Featured on page 120.
O	Owyhee High School	Owyhee, NV	Maintained by the school yearly. Once students painted the O to appear three-dimensional, but later students thought that was too much work, and since then it has been painted white.
O	University of Oregon	Eugene, OR	Built on Skinner Butte in 1908, the O no longer exists. See story and photo on pages 14–15

P CAL POLY
San Luis Obispo, California

Among the rolling hills of the central California coast, the hillside letter P can be seen northwest of U.S. 101 overlooking the Cal Poly campus in San Luis Obispo. The locals call it the Poly P. The P was built in 1919 when California Polytechnic Institute was an all-boys school. The students and administration had considered painting it on a water tower, but that was going to be too expensive. Instead, the letter was made from whitewashed rocks.

When the rocks kept rolling down the hill after the rains, the students rebuilt the P out of old whitewashed barn doors, but it was burned by local high school boys about two years later.

The school rebuilt a temporary P out of wood until a more permanent letter could be constructed. Then in 1939 Harry Wineroth, the student body president, oversaw the construction of the school's first concrete P, with labor provided by the Block P Club, which consisted of young men who had lettered in any of Cal Poly's major sports. The new permanent P's dimensions were 30 feet wide and 40 feet long. The builders applied five hundred gallons of whitewash for its first painting.

The future maintenance of this P was decided by the loser of the Freshman Sophomore Brawl—an annual contest that included greased pole climbs, tugs-of-war, three-legged races, and various other games of skill. Usually the freshmen lost and were responsible for the upkeep of the Poly P. By 1956, the

123

old concrete P was in such disrepair that a group of agricultural engineering students and the Delta Sigma Phi fraternity built another concrete P using supplies donated by local businesses. This 35-by-50-foot monogram, completed May 3, 1957, still watches over the Cal Poly campus today.

At the end of the 1950s the Rally Club began maintaining the P and added a new tradition. The night before the homecoming football game, Rally Club members would drag an old generator up the hill and string lights around the P's outline. If the Poly Mustangs won the game, Rally Club members would change the lights from P to V. The lighting of the P continued until the early 1980s when the Rally Club changed its name to the Running Thunder Club. For the next twelve years or so, the proud Poly P remained dark during homecoming, fell into general disrepair, and became a target of vandals.

In 1994, with the help of the Federal Aviation Administration, the P was stabilized and made an official visual landmark for pilots. The Running Thunder school spirit club began caring for the P. Derek Martin, often referred to as "Mr. P" put in countless hours cleaning, painting, and reinstating the tradition of lighting the P. After Martin retired from his volunteer efforts, the spirit organization decided that what the P needed was someone assigned to look after it. So Running Thunder added a new member to their board—the Keeper of the P.

The Keeper of the P paints the P white several times a year and coordinates the clubs and groups that transform the letter into the colors, symbols, or initials of fraternities, sororities, and other organizations throughout the year. In 2004, the spirit club reorganized under the name Mustang Maniacs. The club lights the P, using a generator and hundreds of Christmas lights, when the football team wins. The lights of this hillside letter can be seen throughout the campus and much of the city.

In addition to being an official FAA landmark, the Poly P has the distinction of being on the National Register of Historic Places, so destroying it would be a federal crime.

Cal Poly's hillside letter, called the Poly P, is on the National Register of Historic Places and is a Federal Aviation Administration landmark.
—COURTESY OF THE *MUSTANG DAILY*, CAL POLY STUDENT NEWSPAPER

Each year the Poly P starts out white, but throughout the year it is painted by various school groups.
—COURTESY OF THE *MUSTANG DAILY*, CAL POLY STUDENT NEWSPAPER

P PORTOLA HIGH SCHOOL
Portola, California

High school students and teachers have come up with some ingenious ways to design hillside letters. In 1935, the freshman class of Portola High School in Portola, California, decided to build a P on Bald Head Mountain southeast of town. The project began under the leadership of their teacher and advisor, Jack Daly. The day they laid out the P on the mountain slope, Daly took with him two students—Dick Janes and Jack Hamilton—and a hundred pounds of old newspapers. Daly and the boys drove as close to the base of the hill as they could get, and then proceeded to climb up the steep mountainside.

After arriving at the chosen location, the three marked the edges of the P's outline using a few large boulders. They covered the letter area with news-

The P on Bald Head Mountain has been cared for by the students of Portola High School for over seven decades. —PHOTO BY DIANA JORGENSON

papers weighed down by small stones. Waiting and watching on the campus below were the rest of the students, who were there to approve the appearance of the letter.

The following morning the freshman class arrived at school wearing old clothes and carrying brooms and buckets from home. The students headed for the base of Bald Head Mountain and began mixing up sacks of whitewash and water in several fifty-gallon drums. After this was done, the freshmen filled their buckets with whitewash and carried them up to the newspaper P. There they replaced the newspaper with small rocks and applied the first coat of whitewash to their hillside letter.

Since 1998 the P has been painted instead of whitewashed. The P is maintained every four years, so every student gets a chance to participate in the painting of the P at least once.

	NAME	LOCATION	NOTE
P	Cal Poly	San Luis Obispo, CA	Featured on page 123.
P	Page	Page, AZ	The P was painted in 1960 on red sandstone bluffs just outside of town. In 2004 students at Page High School carefully cleaned off many years of written class years so the solitary P would once again stand out. See photo on page 10.
P	Pahranagat Valley High School	Alamo, NV	This small school of about ninety students maintains its letter once every four years, so that all students get a chance to paint the P during their high school years.
P	Paisley	Paisley, OR	The seniors of Paisley High School care for this community letter and add their graduating year alongside it.
P	Palisade High School	Palisade, CO	The freshmen, under the direction of the seniors, paint the Palisade P each year as part of their homecoming activities
P	Palomar College	San Marcos, CA	Seven students—Bill Tipton, Alden Avery, Dick Golem, Kenny Sims, Lionel Moore, Ken Staller, and John Trexel—were responsible for building the P, which is maintained regularly.

	NAME	LOCATION	NOTE
P	Paonia High School	Paonia, CO	Whitewashed annually by the student council.
P	Park High School	Livingston, MT	Made of whitewashed rocks and maintained by community groups such as the Boy Scouts and the chamber of commerce.
P	Parker	Parker, AZ	Visible but no longer maintained.
P	Parowan High School	Parowan, UT	Each year just before graduation, the seniors clean and whitewash their hillside P. Then on the night of graduation, two teachers hike up the hill with flares and light the P to honor the graduating seniors.
P	Payson High School	Payson, UT	Each year in the spring, the juniors ascend the hillside to paint the P.
PHOENIX	Phoenix	Mesa, AZ	Featured on page 183.
P	Piute High School	Junction, UT	The senior class paints the rock P and adds their graduating year next to it.
P	Plains	Plains, MT	The rock P represents both the community and the combined Plains School; it is whitewashed by the student council.
P	Pleasant Grove	Pleasant Grove, UT	Because the P stands for both the community and Pleasant Grove High School, the two parties join together to maintain and whitewash the letters.
P	Pocatello	Pocatello, ID	This community letter located on the West Bench is maintained by the students of Pocatello High School during homecoming week.
P	Pojoaque	Pojoaque, NM	The P representing this pueblo community near Santa Fe is maintained by the residents.
P	Polson	Polson, MT	Representing both Polson High School and the community, the P is maintained by the high school key club.
P	Pomona College	Claremont, CA	The letter was built in 1912. The Pomona College handbook of 1915–1916 reads: "The Associated Students passed a resolution to the effect that it shall be the privilege and duty of each incoming Freshman Class to free the surface of the letter from brush, to put a row of rocks, firmly placed, one foot wide around the letter, and to make white all the rocks placed up to that time." This tradition was upheld until the P was removed shortly after World War II.
P	Portola High School	Portola, CA	Featured on page 126.
P	Powell County High School	Deer Lodge, MT	Maintained by the students.
PC	Prairie City High School	Prairie City, OR	Painted each year by the incoming freshmen.
P	Prescott	Prescott, AZ	Represents both Prescott High School and the community; painted white each year by the student council and alumni.
P	Preston	Preston, ID	Represents both Preston High School and the community. The high school shop class constructed the P of concrete pavers framed with metal edging, and various athletic groups whitewash it annually.

Q QUARTZSITE
Quartzsite, Arizona

If you ever drive along the dry, flat desert that stretches from Phoenix to Los Angeles on Interstate 10, you can't miss the hillside Q seventeen miles east of the California border. About twelve youths and their parents designed, built, and painted the Q for Quartzsite, Arizona, back in the early 1950s.

Presently, Quartzsite has a little over three thousand year-round residents, but in the 1950s and 1960s there were only about sixty-five. Today, over a million people make Quartzsite their home during the winter. That's a lot of houseguests! These "snowbirds" keep Quartzsite busy by attending the local rock and mineral shows, exchanging their handmade goods at the numerous swap meets, sweeping the nearby desert with their metal detectors for buried treasure, or just camping out in their RVs and enjoying the warm winter weather of Arizona.

However, back in 1953, the town was so small that it had no school. So the board of education gave the community a small bus that held about eight students, and they would ride to nearby towns such as Salome, Parker, or Ehrenberg for school. Even though the students didn't have a school in their hometown, they wanted a hillside letter like the ones they had seen in other places. The idea of building a Q for Quartzsite became an important topic among the students riding on the bus. Finally the students presented the idea to their parents, explaining that they wanted to build a giant Q out of quartz

The hillside letter on Q Mountain was built by the children of Quartzsite, Arizona, in 1953.
—PHOTO BY JAMES J. PARSONS; COURTESY OF PAUL F. STARRS, UNIVERSITY OF NEVADA–RENO

for their town. The parents agreed, and the group selected a prominent cone-shaped hill just south of town, today known as Q Mountain.

Rosalee Wheeler, one of the mothers involved with the project, remembers that everyone helped—even the preschool children. They began by drawing the shape of the letter on the hill with powdered lime. Then they placed pieces of quartz, large and small (depending on the size a child could carry) along the outline. Soon a large built-up Q began taking shape on the hillside. After all the quartz was in place, the children mixed up whitewash in large wash tubs they had brought from home and poured it over the quartz. It wasn't the neatest job, but the children were pretty proud of what they had accomplished. When they were done, the tired, whitewash-splattered group climbed down the hill to take a look at the new emblem, never realizing what an important landmark it would become.

Quartzsite's hillside Q appears on the town logo.
—COURTESY OF THE TOWN OF QUARTZSITE

A year or so later, Barry Goldwater, Arizona's new U.S. senator, was flying over the area and noticed Quartzsite's new emblem. From the air, he could see that one side of the Q was quite lopsided. After making inquiries, Senator Goldwater wrote the children a letter explaining the problem he had seen and included twenty-five dollars for them to fix it. The children and their parents purchased more whitewash with the money, and then did their best to fix the lopsided Q.

Over the years members of the community—even the snowbirds—have donated money towards maintenance of the Q, which has come to be a significant symbol of identity for the town. A new subdivision and various businesses use the name Q Mountain, and the image of the Q on the hill is even part of Quartzsite's town logo.

	NAME	LOCATION	NOTE
Q	Quartzsite	Quartzsite, AZ	Featured on page 129.
Q	Questa	Questa, NM	The Q represents both Questa High School and the community. The students paint it each year to keep it looking bright.
Q	Quincy	Quincy, CA	A community letter.

R RICKS COLLEGE (BRIGHAM YOUNG UNIVERSITY–IDAHO)
Rexburg, Idaho

Sometimes hillside letters are abandoned. That is what happened to the R overlooking Rexburg, Idaho, a small college town in eastern Idaho about fifty miles west of the Grand Teton Mountains. The whitewashed R, which is one of about twenty-nine letters in Idaho, isn't for Rexburg, but rather for Ricks College.

Ricks began as an academy in 1888, then in 1923 became Ricks College. During the early days the school struggled financially. Its first principal, Jacob Spori, gave up a portion of his salary, and faculty members agreed to receive part of their pay in produce rather than cash to help pay the bills of this struggling institution. As time went on, not only did the school overcome its financial difficulties, but its enrollment made it the nation's largest private two-year college until it became a four-year school.

In 1962 the homecoming theme for Ricks College was "New Horizons." To celebrate the theme, math teacher Harold Nielsen thought the school should paint a giant R on North Menan Butte about six miles west of town, where it would be visible on the horizon. The school's athletic director, Don Rydalch, and the math club, called the Mathletes, set aside October 13 as the day they would build and paint the R. The club members asked for assistance from the rest of the student body because the letter was designed to be as large as a

Ricks College students painting their giant rock R. The old emblem was abandoned in 2001 when the name of the school changed to Brigham Young University–Idaho, but the R is still visible.

—PHOTO BY MICHAEL LEWIS; COURTESY OF BRIGHAM YOUNG UNIVERSITY–DAHO

football field. The college administration helped by providing buses for travel between the campus and the butte.

North Menan Butte, like its twin to the south, is part of a volcanic field, so there were plenty of basalt rocks for a built-up letter. In spite of all the work, the football team unfortunately lost the homecoming game of 1962; but the school gained a new landmark and a new tradition of painting and lighting the R for each homecoming.

In 2001, Ricks College, which is owned by the Mormon Church, was renamed Brigham Young University–Idaho and became a four-year institution. Because of this name change, the college decided not to maintain the R and is letting the site return to its natural state. Since that time, the students at Brigham Young University–Idaho like to remind people that while they may have a new name, they still have "the spirit of Ricks" in their hearts. So even though the

R on the butte has been abandoned and will eventually fade away, the students believe the spirit of the old letter will never die.

R UNIVERSITY OF REDLANDS
Redlands, California

In 1913, the students of the University of Redlands built a cutout letter R that has stood the test of time. There are only a handful of cutout letters in the nation, and the R on Mount Harrison, just to the north of campus and overlooking the community of Redlands, California, is the best example.

The R is located on San Bernardino National Forest land, about ten miles from the University of Redlands campus. When the letter was built, U.S. For-

Snow filling in the giant cutout R creates a prominent landmark for the University of Redlands.
—PHOTO BY GREG SCHNEIDER

134

est Service rangers supervised its construction. For a number of years after it was built, the R was lighted during homecoming by tracing its outline in railroad flares. In 1926 the U.S. Forest Service informed the university that it could no longer use the property on which the R was located. The university immediately protested, and after some negotiations the Forest Service allowed the R to remain, but the lighting of the letter had to cease because it posed a fire hazard. The Forest Service also required that the shape and size of the letter not be changed by clearing more brush, and the letter must never be painted or concreted.

The R is a truly giant letter. Because it is a cutout letter the R size has varied, from approximately 320 to 275 feet wide and 460 to 415 feet long. On February 22, 1958, Redland's University Day, Dave Dunning measured the R at 275 feet wide and 415 feet long. These measurements make the R the second-longest letter in the nation (after Western State College's W) and the largest cutout letter ever made. Nearly a century old, and at an elevation of 4,743 feet above sea level, the old cutout R requires frequent weeding, which keeps the University of Redlands Bulldogs busy.

	NAME	LOCATION	NOTE
R	Randsburg	Randsburg, CA	Randsburg is a "living ghost town" with only about eighty residents, but that is enough to give the old R a new coat of paint whenever it is needed.
R	Ray	Ray, AZ	There was once a hillside R that represented the mining community of Ray, but the town and the letter no longer exist due to expansion of the mine.
R	Ray High School	Kearny, AZ	The seniors paint the rock R, adding the first two numbers of their class year before the letter, and the last two numbers after it.
RL	Red Lodge	Red Lodge, MT	Representing both Red Lodge High School and the community, the RL is cared for by the high school students.

	NAME	LOCATION	NOTE
R	Reed High School	Sparks, NV	Various student groups whitewash the giant R each year.
R	Reedley	Reedley, CA	This letter is maintained and is visible; however, it is unknown who is responsible for it.
R	Reno High School	Reno, NV	No longer exists.
R	Richfield High School	Richfield, UT	The whitewashed R is cared for by the students.
R	Ricks College (Brigham Young University–Idaho)	Rexburg, ID	Featured on page 132.
R	Roberts	Roberts, MT	A rock letter representing both Robert's High School and the community; maintained and painted white by the senior class.
R	Robertson High School	Las Vegas, NM	Maintained by the seniors each year.
RHS	Rock Springs High School	Rock Springs, WY	No longer exists.
R	Rockland High School	Rockland, ID	Maintained by members of the senior class.
RM	Rocky Mountain High School	Byron, WY	The RM replaced a hillside B in the mid-1980s when Byron High School closed.
R	Rogue River High School	Rogue River, OR	When the R was first cut out of the trees, it was difficult to see except when the snow fell, but since then students have filled in the cutout R with white vinyl, and it stands out year round. This letter is rarely cared for because it is surrounded by poison oak, keeping it well protected from rivals but also from students who try to maintain it.
R	Rosalia High School	Rosalia, WA	The R was built in 2003 and is maintained by the students.
R	Rosebud	Rosebud, MT	A school and community letter made of bricks, which the seniors and freshmen of Rosebud High School whitewash each year.
RV	Round Valley High School	Eager, AZ	The students built their hillside RV. It is whitewashed once a year for homecoming.
R	Roundup High School	Roundup, MT	The students spend one day each year cleaning up the community and doing service projects; often this includes repainting the rock R.
R	Roy	Roy, MT	The rock R stands for both Roy High School and the community. The senior class maintains and whitewashes it on an as-needed basis.
R	Ryegate	Ryegate, MT	The community of Ryegate and Ryegate K–12 School District maintain and whitewash this hillside R.
R	St. Regis High School	St Regis, MT	The R is made of tires, and it is painted white by the junior and senior classes each year for homecoming.
R	University of Redlands	Redlands, CA	Featured on page 134.

SALOME
Salome, Arizona

Have you ever swung a bat and missed the ball, then heard someone say, "You missed that by a mile"? That's what happened to Charles W. Pratt, the founder of Salome, Arizona, a rural community of nearly two thousand people located in the McMullen Valley of western Arizona on Route 60. In 1904, Pratt guessed where the coming railroad might lay its tracks and established the community of Salome, only to find out he had missed the location by a mile. The town had to be moved in order to be located on the Arizona & California Railroad line.

Even near the railroad, Salome struggled to grow. Finally, after more than fifty years, the town built its first high school in 1955. Three years later, the small but enthusiastic student body and faculty of Salome High School constructed a rock S by hand. Mo Montijo and some of his fellow classmates built the letter by first rolling out white butcher paper in the shape of an S. Without cell phones or walkie-talkies to communicate, the teachers used hand signals from the road below to help the students lay out the paper S correctly. Once they had the shape, they built up the S with rocks and whitewashed it.

More than half a century later, the letterman club of Salome's Fighting Frogs paints and cares for the emblem. Today the S is considered a community letter, a hometown landmark that has come to represent the town of Salome.

Salome's S is maintained by the students of Salome High School. —PHOTO
BY JAMES J. PARSONS; COURTESY OF PAUL F. STARRS, UNIVERSITY OF NEVADA–RENO

The young men of Snow College built this S in 1926 after waiting more than a decade
for approval from the school. —COURTESY OF SNOW COLLEGE ALUMNI ASSOCIATION

SNOW COLLEGE
Ephraim, Utah

Since about 1914, students of Snow Academy, a small school in Ephraim, Utah, had been talking about building a school letter on the hillside above their school, as many other schools and communities in Utah had already done. The letters SA had earlier been constructed of concrete and placed on the front of the gym. However, since their removal in 1914, the students had been eyeing a spot on the mountain overlooking the school. For the next eleven years the students and school administration discussed the idea of building an S on the hillside. In the October 28, 1925, edition of the *Snowdrift*, the student newspaper, this poem was printed:

> The rumor's going around the school
> It's passed from John to Phil.
> When will we get a block "S"
> Placed upon the hill?

A committee of students, faculty, and alumni formed to select a site and design the letter, but not much more could be done because by then Snow College and the proposed site were covered in a heavy blanket of snow. The students waited out the winter, and on May 3, 1926, the senior boys began clearing the designated slope of undergrowth to make way for the 150-foot-wide and 250-foot-long S. After they had cleared the site, the boys outlined a giant S with rocks. This work was completed on May 20, and the tired young men headed down the hillside to enjoy the picnic the girls had prepared for them to celebrate their accomplishment.

The following year the outlined S was filled in with rocks and whitewashed for the school's Founders Day celebration. The student body, faculty, alumni and the townspeople of Ephraim had gathered on the evening of Founders Day for some traditional activities, when to the surprise of many the S broke into flames. Unknown to everyone, the freshmen had secretly planned and

139

The 1930 Snow College yearbook included this photo of the school's four-year-old hillside emblem.

—COURTESY OF SNOW COLLEGE ALUMNI ASSOCIATION

executed the lighting of the S, which was an instant success and has become a Founders Day tradition. However, the lighting was afterwards assigned to the upperclassmen rather than to the nervy freshmen.

For the students of the school as well as the community of Ephraim, Utah, the hillside S represents the spirit of Snow College, and after more than three-quarters of a century it has become a hometown landmark.

SMD SOUTH DAKOTA SCHOOL OF MINES AND TECHNOLOGY
Rapid City, South Dakota

Founded in 1876 by gold prospectors, the community of Rapid City, South Dakota, has grown from a popular watering hole to a beautiful city. If you visit Rapid City—referred to by locals as Rapid—you will see a three-letter emblem on a hillside overlooking the area. The SMD is on Cowboy Hill, the first ridge of the Black Hills just west of town. In 1912, the students of the South Dakota School of Mines, now known as South Dakota School of Mines and Technology, began construction of the letter M. At that time it was the easternmost collegiate hillside letter in the nation. The addition of South Dakota's M to the ten hillside letters that then existed meant that half of all letters were Ms, thanks to two other mining schools and two Montana schools. Today the letter M is still the most prevalent hillside letter.

President O'Harra of the School of Mines declared a school holiday called M Day on October 5, 1912, to allow time for the building of the M. Sixty-five male students and ten faculty members packed themselves a sack lunch, gathered tools, and made their way up Cowboy Hill. There they surveyed the hillside and laid out the M. With their markings the mining students began

Students and faculty of the South Dakota School of Mines ascend Cowboy Hill for M Day, a favorite tradition. —COURTESTY OF THE SOUTH DATKOTA SCHOOL OF MINES AND TECHNOLOGY, OFFICE OF UNIVERSITY RELATIONS

the excavation of their monogram by plowing up the soil in the outline of an M. Using picks, shovels, and two teams of horse-drawn plows with wagons attached, one group loosened the soil and threw it in the back of the wagon to be hauled away. Another group filled in the newly dug trenches with stones. According to historical accounts, some one hundred wagonloads of rock were required to build the 67-foot-wide, 112.5-foot-long M.

What did the good folks of Rapid think of this? The 1912 *Black Hills Weekly Journal* reported that many curious townspeople could be seen with their spyglasses, opera glasses, or binoculars viewing the unusual proceedings on Cowboy Hill. When the M was completed, folks said the whitewashed letter could be seen as far as twelve miles away.

For more than ninety years students and faculty have been celebrating homecoming week, called M Week, each September with picnics, a bonfire, a homecoming parade, and a coronation of homecoming royalty. On Friday afternoon of M Week, classes are canceled for the painting of the M. The seniors escort the freshmen—referred to as "froshmen" until they are officially recognized by the seniors at half-time during the homecoming football game—from the campus to M Hill, a walk of several miles. The froshmen wear strange clothes and green beanies with a yellow M, while the seniors wear what look like old mining caps, which are covered with the signatures of friends and teachers.

Through the years, the students have added new traditions to the M Week festivities. In 1922 the rock M was partially replaced by concrete, and the seniors began a tradition (skipped in 1923) of embedding into the concrete a bronze plaque displaying their class year, names, and degrees. At that time they stamped into the concrete the years 1913 through 1921 to honor previous classes. The students also began a tradition of making a giant mudslide on the hill and sliding down from the letter to the base; since the 1980s they slide down the letter's wet painted surface instead. During M Week of 1953, the students constructed a concrete S and D on either side of the M.

In 1913 these students from the South Dakota School of Mines prepared to whitewash their hillside M for its first anniversary. —ALUMNI COLLECTION ARCHIVES OF DEVEREAUX LIBRARY, SOUTH DAKOTA SCHOOL OF MINES AND TECHNOLOGY

From 1912 until 1952 the hillside M captured in this 1915 photo graced the slopes of Cowboy Hill. In 1953 the Miners added the letters S and D on either side of the M. —ALUMNI COLLECTION ARCHIVES OF DEVEREAUX LIBRARY, SOUTH DAKOTA SCHOOL OF MINES AND TECHNOLOGY

Every five years the school celebrates a reunion welcoming all alumni back to campus. The favorite activity of the reunion is the M Climb, in which former students take spouses, children, and grandchildren up Cowboy Hill to find their names on their class plaque. Those who are not physically able to make the trek to the letters are transported by the school.

In October 2006, much of the undeveloped land on Cowboy Hill was sold at auction with plans to build homes, commercial businesses, and a city park. However, before selling the land, the owners of the property set aside a green belt around the SMD, keeping this hometown landmark protected for decades to come.

SR SUL ROSS STATE UNIVERSITY
Alpine, Texas

The letters SR overlooking the campus of Sul Ross State University were built in 1925, only five years after the school first opened its doors. The school, located in Alpine, Texas, in the center of the panhandle, was named for Lawrence Sullivan Ross, a Texas ranger, Civil War hero, and governor of Texas. Sul Ross State Normal College was created in 1917 by an act of the Texas legislature as a college to train teachers. The residents of Alpine were asked to provide the land, the utilities for the college, and the housing for the students. The legislature would provide $200,000 for buildings and equipment.

When the school began three years later, it consisted of seventy-seven students and a single building. However, by the summer of 1925, the school had added enough advanced courses to award its first baccalaureate degree under its new name: Sul Ross State Teachers College. Also during that year the students of Sul Ross built their hillside emblem on the foothills of the Davis Mountains northeast of the school.

Sul Ross State University's hillside SR in Alpine, Texas, was built in 1925 in the image of the school's registered cattle brand, the Bar-SR-Bar. —PHOTO BY NANCY BLANTON, SUL ROSS STATE UNIVERSITY NEWS AND PUBLICATIONS

Since most of the residents of western Texas during that time were cattlemen, their donations to the school didn't come in the form of cash, but rather in calves. In 1921, Sul Ross registered the Bar-SR-Bar brand (which appears as an SR with horizontal bars above and below), and all calves donated were branded and added to the school's scholarship fund. The Bar-SR-Bar was also added to the cover of the school's first yearbook, the *Brand*, and the school's letterhead. Both of these traditions continue today. Consequently, when the students proposed building a hillside landmark for their school, it wasn't surprising that they chose an image of the brand.

The whitewashed rock Bar-SR-Bar stands about seventy-five feet across and seventy-five feet long. It is maintained and painted annually under the direction of the school's Student Life Office, and it is lighted with torches for homecoming each fall. These events are among many "Bar-SR-Bar traditions" in which the school encourages students to participate.

The Sul Ross State University emblem is unique among hillside letters in that it is a registered cattle brand that is still used by the school in branding its livestock. (The D in Duarte, California, also a brand, is no longer in use.) The Bar-SR-Bar stands as a reminder of the contributions the early citizens of Alpine, Texas, were willing to make for the education of Texas children.

	NAME	LOCATION	NOTE
SH	Sacred Heart High School	San Francisco, CA	The letters no longer exist.
S	Saguache	Saguache, CO	The S was originally built for Saguache High School and the community; however, the old high school closed and the students now attend Mountain Valley Senior High School. The students still care for the community's hillside S.
S	Salida	Salida, CO	The concrete S is a community letter and is maintained by the residents.
S	Salmon High School	Salmon, ID	The seniors whitewash the S and add their graduation year next to it.
S	Salome	Salome, AZ	Featured on page 137.
S	San Diego State University	San Diego, CA	The rock S, representing what was then San Diego State College, was built in 1931 on Cowles Mountain a little northeast of campus. It was maintained by the freshmen, who would clear it of vegetation and repaint it. Sometime during the 1980s it became an environmental issue and the school abandoned it. After a recent wildfire burned away the brush, the S became visible for a brief time, but it has since become hidden by vegetation.
S	San Jacinto	San Jacinto, CA	The S on the face of San Jacinto Mountain was built by the Boy Scouts sometime during the 1930s. The S stands for both the community and San Jacinto High School, just north the letter.

146

	NAME	LOCATION	NOTE
SL	San Luis Obispo High School	San Luis Obispo, CA	Cared for by the high school's Future Farmers of America chapter.
S	Sanderson	Sanderson, TX	This community letter represents and is maintained by the people of Sanderson, the "cactus capital" of Texas.
S	Sanford Public School	Sanford, CO	The students of this small K–12 school whitewash their S each year during Spirit Week.
S	Sanger	Sanger, CA	Maintained by Sanger High School and the community.
S	Seligman High School	Seligman, AZ	The S is painted white as part of the school's homecoming activities, and when the students are feeling patriotic they paint it red, white, and blue.
S	Sentinel High School	Missoula, MT	Removed.
S	Shafter	Shafter, TX	Represents the community of about eighty residents.
S	Shandon High/ Middle School	Shandon, CA	Cared for by the students.
S	Shelby High School	Shelby, MT	The first S for Shelby High School was built in 1940s in the north part of town. The current S was built about 1990 behind the school, and it is maintained and whitewashed by the freshman and senior classes as part of homecoming activities.
SB	Sierra Blanca	Sierra Blanca, TX	The SB is not maintained.
SV	Silver Valley High School	Yermo, CA	Occasionally maintained by the students.
SV	Sky View High School	Smithfield, UT	The whitewashed rock SV is cared for by the school.
S	Skyline High School	Salt Lake City, UT	The students paint the S each year during homecoming.
SV	Smith Valley Schools	Smith, NV	The SV represents Smith Valley Schools as well as the Smith Valley community, which includes the towns of Smith and Wellington. The SV is visible throughout the valley and is painted by the letterman club of the school once every other year.
S	Snow College	Ephraim, UT	Featured on page 139.
SMD	South Dakota School of Mines and Technology	Rapid City, SD	Featured on page 140.

147

	NAME	LOCATION	NOTE
SS	South Sevier High School	Monroe, UT	The SS near Monroe is a challenge to reach, but it is maintained once a year during homecoming and lighted with flares during the game.
SWC	South Wasco County High School	Maupin, OR	Each year the senior class spruces up their white rock SWC and adds their graduation year below it.
S	Sparks	Sparks, NV	Built in 1925, the white S above Sparks is still maintained by the community.
SJ	St. Johns	St. Johns, AZ	The SJ represents both the community and St. Johns High School; the student council regularly maintains the letters and paints them white.
SMC	St. Mary's College of California	Moraga, CA	The brick SMC that has been on the campus since about 1927 has become a sort of student message board. Each year when school starts the three-lettered emblem is painted white, and during the year student groups paint over the letters with symbols, words, and colors identifying their clubs. When the students leave in the summer the SMC is again painted white.
S	Stanford High School	Stanford, MT	The seniors and freshmen whitewash their S as part of the freshman initiation.
S	Sterling	Sterling, UT	No longer maintained but visible.
S	Stewart Indian School	Carson City, NV	Students of the Stewart Indian School, which operated from 1890 to 1980, built a rock S that is still visible, but very faint, on Snyder Avenue one mile east of U.S. 395.
SR	Sul Ross State University	Alpine, TX	Featured on page 144.
S	Sunnyslope High School	Phoenix, AZ	The high school student council leads the freshmen to the S each year to whitewash it, accompanied by local firemen who also help out.
S	Superior	Superior, AZ	The S is considered a community letter, but the seniors of Superior High School maintain and light it for homecoming and graduation using small pots filled with fuel.
S	Superior High School	Superior, MT	Painted by the juniors, who add their class year next to it.

T THERMOPOLIS
Thermopolis, Wyoming

The community of Thermopolis in central Wyoming is known for its white-water rafting down nearby Wind River Canyon and for hosting the world's largest mineral hot springs. This attractive town on the Bighorn River is home to a letter T, located in Hot Springs State Park on the south side of T Hill. Like most small communities with a hillside letter, Thermopolis has no written history of its T. Even local historians and old-timers don't know what inspired the residents of Thermopolis to build a hillside emblem; however, it appeared around the time the local high school opened. Older townsfolk do recall that before the letter was on the hill, a wild elk was kept penned there. The T appeared on what was then Elk Hill, now known as T Hill, shortly after the first high school was built in 1921. No one recalls what happened to the elk.

The freshmen at Hot Springs High School traditionally painted the T as their initiation into school, and nothing of note seems to have occurred until the fall of 1998, when the junior class rearranged the rocks of the T into the numbers 1999, their graduating year. Their actions caused an immediate outcry from other students and community residents. The juniors were told to return the T to its original condition, but instead they changed it into a peace symbol. This did not create peace in Thermopolis, as evidenced by the outpouring of mail to the editor of the local newspaper. Even though residents

The whitewashed rock T stands out against the red foothills of Thermopolis, Wyoming.
—PHOTO BY RICHARD COFFINBERRY

did not know why they had a hillside letter, they knew they wanted it back. Shortly afterwards, the T was returned to its original condition.

Today, the whitewashed rock T still stands out against the rocky hillsides of Thermopolis. During the summer, a herd of buffalo belonging to the state park graze nearby. The Boy Scouts of America and other service groups make sure the rock T is maintained and unchanged, because in Thermopolis—as in other small towns of the West—hillside letter traditions are important, even if no one knows why.

T TINTIC HIGH SCHOOL
Eureka, Utah

The oldest high school hillside letter is the T in the small town of Eureka, Utah, visible just south of U.S. 6 about seventy miles southwest of Salt Lake City. Eureka began as a mining community. In the late 1800s it became the financial center of the Tintic Mining District, at one time one of the top mineral-producing areas in the state. Today this community of about seven hundred people no longer consists of miners, but the schools still carry the Tintic name.

Built in 1912, the T for Tintic High School in Eureka, Utah, was the first high school hillside letter in the nation.
—THOMAS E. NEDREBERG, TINTIC HIGH SCHOOL

Since 1949, each graduating class of Tintic High School has placed a plaque referred to as "senior letters" in the concrete T. —THOMAS E. NEDREBERG, TINTIC HIGH SCHOOL

The students of Tintic High School built the T in the spring of 1912, just a few months before Eureka's first high school building was completed. The young builders of the T may have been influenced by the giant hillside Y in Provo, Utah, which had been built for Brigham Young University six years earlier and was visible a few miles from Eureka. The students first built their T by outlining it with rocks. A year later Tintic High School and the community celebrated the first anniversary of T-Day, and they have celebrated it every year since.

For nearly a century, the traditions of T-Day haven't changed much. On the night before T-Day, the letter is lighted—in the past with burning bags of sawdust and today with electric lights. In town, the students and community members used to gather around a bonfire to sing the school song and reminisce; this tradition has been replaced with a school carnival for the community. The next morning, the seniors take all the male students up to the T to whitewash it and to clean the hillside, while the senior girls organize the rest of the female students in cleaning the school and preparing lunch.

Over the years, the students of Tintic High School have reinforced the rocks of the T with concrete. For T-Day each year the senior class, which varies in size from fifteen to twenty students, embeds in the T a plaque referred to as "senior letters," which contains the class year and the names or initials of the class members and their advisor. This graduation tradition began over half a century ago; the oldest metal plaque is dated 1949. Today if you visit the T, you can see a variety of handmade class plaques. Many are three-dimensional and most are made from metal, thanks to the help of Jay Evans, the shop teacher and resident historian of the T.

Tintic's T is approximately 45 feet wide and 65 feet long. Most years it is painted white, but in 2002, when a Salt Lake City radio station encouraged local Utah schools to paint their hillside emblems with red, white, and blue stripes as a sign of support to soldiers flying out of Utah, Tintic students showed their colors.

T TROPIC
Tropic, Utah

Each year over 1.5 million people travel to Bryce Canyon National Park, at the eastern edge of the Paunsaugunt Plateau in southern Utah, to see the beautiful limestone amphitheaters and the tall, colorful hoodoos that fill the horseshoe-shaped canyon. Some of these visitors might be curious about the little town they see nestled in the valley to the east below the rim.

The T just south of Tropic, Utah, was built by the senior class of Tropic High School in about 1931 and was restored in 1997. —PHOTO BY JIM CORNING

While the rim along Bryce Canyon can get very cold and windy, the climate in the valley below is more suitable for habitation; however, when settlers first arrived the valley lacked sufficient water for their needs. In 1890 and 1891, some of the industrious early residents of this area dug a ten-mile-long irrigation ditch over the east rim of Bryce Canyon. This channel carried water from the East Fork of the Sevier River 1,500 feet down to the valley floor. The settlers' hard work paid off, and they were able to plant gardens and grow orchards. Hence the residents named their town Tropic.

In 1922, an old, abandoned store building was converted into the first high school, providing classes up to tenth grade. Students from two neighboring towns, Henrieville, and Cannonville, also attended school in the old store.

The old Tropic High School had no electricity and the only heat came from two potbellied stoves, one upstairs and the other down. When enrollment increased, eleventh and twelfth grade were added, as well as electricity.

Sometime around 1931 the senior class built a rock T, 42 feet wide by 34 feet long, on a hill just south of town. For a number of years, the senior class whitewashed this T the night before graduation, using brooms and brushes brought from home. But eventually the whole school got involved, and everyone enjoyed Tropic High School's T Party, which included large dishpans filled to the brim with homemade potato salad, plates piled high with sandwiches and hot dogs, and a ten-gallon can of homemade root beer or punch.

In December 1953, the old Tropic High School caught fire. There was only one phone in town, and in the excitement Mable Ott, who telephoned the out-of-town operator to report the fire, forgot to mention that the fire was in Tropic. The town had no fire department and the locals had only garden hoses to fight the fire, so the fire quickly consumed the building. According to Ella Adair, a teacher at the school, "It was an emotional experience, as a helpless community stood and watched their beloved school reduced to ashes. Years of memories went up in smoke." However, the community and church rallied, and within a day or so classes were being held in four different buildings. The theme of the following two years was "The Town is Our Campus."

In 1955, the students of the old Tropic High School had a new building with a new name—Bryce Valley High School. Two years later the students at the new high school placed a large BV on the foothills east of town. The old T was abandoned, and the freshman class began maintaining the new BV.

In 1996 the old Tropic High School classes of 1952 and 1953, the last two classes to graduate from the school before it burned, planned their high school reunion. Their old hillside T had completely disappeared from view in the forty-five years since graduation. The loss of this hometown landmark was unacceptable, so the group enlisted the help of one of their classmates still living in Tropic, Lowell Mecham. Donating fifty dollars to the cause, the class

The BV just east of Tropic, Utah, stands for Bryce Valley High School and is painted and lighted annually. —PHOTO BY JIM CORNING

members asked Mecham to see if he could find any remains of their school emblem and rebuild it for their upcoming reunion.

It took some searching, but Mecham is not a man who gives up, and he eventually was able to find a few scattered whitewashed rocks near the old site. Mecham enlisted the help of his son, who brought his family and two friends to help rebuild and whitewash the T. By July of 1997, just in time for the reunion, the old landmark T was once again visible over Tropic.

In 1998, the students of Bryce Valley High School moved into a new high school building and turned the old building over to Bryce Valley Elementary School. With supervision from the senior class the freshman students still whitewash and maintain the BV, and they light it for high school graduation. The T is maintained by the community.

TB TWIN BRIDGES HIGH SCHOOL
Twin Bridges, Montana

The town of Twin Bridges, Montana, in the southwestern corner of the state, gets its name from the bridges located at each end of town. Just outside of Twin Bridges, the Ruby and Big Hole Rivers meet together with the Beaverhead to form the Jefferson River. This fishermen's paradise is one of the water routes traveled by the Lewis and Clark expedition in 1805 as they searched for the family and tribe of their female Indian guide, Sacajawea, on whom they were counting to provide them with much-needed horses. Near Twin Bridges Sacajawea recognized a landmark she called the "Beaver-head," indicating her homeland was nearby.

For many years students at Twin Bridges High School wanted a landmark to announce their hometown to travelers along Montana Highway 41. However it wasn't until the 1992-1993 school year that senior Trent Gibson decided that the students of Twin Bridges High School had waited long enough. In fact, he declared, he wasn't going to graduate until this happened. Gibson was the president of the Family, Career, and Community Leaders of America (FCCLA) at Twin Bridges High School, so he presented his idea to the school chapter of the FCCLA and to his advisor Janice Denson, a teacher at the school. Both agreed to support him in his efforts.

The group hadn't done anything like this before, but that didn't stop the energetic students and their advisor. First they learned how to use surveying equipment, and then they obtained permission to put the letters TB on the property of the Jefferson Cattle Company. Steve Swan, an alumnus of Twin Bridges High School and owner of a concrete company, donated four thousand dollars worth of concrete for the project. After staking out the two letters about a mile north of town on the foothills of the Tobacco Root Mountains, the students built forms outlining the letters TB and removed rocks to allow a smoother application of concrete. Then they found out that it would take less concrete if the rocks were left in, so they put the rocks back in the forms.

This photo hangs in the entryway of Twin Bridges High School. —COURTESY OF TWIN BRIDGES SCHOOLS

When the day for the big pour arrived, the cement truck couldn't get close enough to the letters, so the determined students applied the concrete the old fashioned way: by bucket brigade. Twenty-one students and three adults from the school hauled, troweled, and finished the concrete TB. When the job was completed, Denson told the students to inscribe their initials somewhere on the wet concrete, so that someday they could return and tell their children and grandchildren how they had helped construct the TB.

Later that year all the students in town, kindergarten through twelfth grade, were bused to the site of the new landmark for a dedication ceremony. Four hundred or so residents of Twin Bridges also attended. Trent Gibson led the ceremony. A local couple, Jim and Betty Sykes, along with their granddaughter Carlena, gave the concrete TB a final coat of sealer to ensure that the letter would be well preserved.

To commemorate this event, the school had a poster-sized photo of the TB made, which hangs in the display case of the new high school. The freshmen at Twin Bridges High School annually paint the letters and clean up around the site.

158

	NAME	LOCATION	NOTE
T	Fort Thomas	Fort Thomas, AZ	The T is on government property and is maintained by service organizations such as the Boy Scouts.
T	Tempe	Tempe, AZ	The rock T on a small butte is visible but not regularly maintained.
T	Templeton	Templeton, CA	A large white T that is currently maintained.
T	Ten Sheep	Ten Sheep, WY	Made of rock; visible but no longer painted.
T	Thermopolis	Thermopolis, WY	Featured on page 149.
T	Throop College of Technology (Caltech)	Pasadena, CA	On Christmas Day 1915, students and two professors cut out a giant T, for Tech, on the face of Mount Wilson. The freshman class cleared brush from the letter during their annual "T Party." The letter was immortalized in song, and in 1923 the school yearbook, *The Big T*, included this tribute: "Long may the Big T on the mountainside continue to blazon forth its message from the heart of Tech to all mankind. Long may it stand for Truth, a Testament to Tech." By 1929, the U.S. Forest Service halted any further maintenance of the T because of erosion, and it has disappeared from view.
T	Thunderbird High School	Phoenix, AZ	A white rock letter.
T	Tigers of Hot Springs High School	Truth or Consequences, NM	The seniors paint the rock T on Turtleback Mountain.
T	Tintic High School	Eureka, UT	Featured on page 151.
T	Tombstone	Tombstone, AZ	The letter on T Hill is considered both a school and a community letter; the Tombstone High School Varsity Club paints it annually.
T	Tonopah High School	Tonopah, NV	The T was built in 1917 to honor the girls' basketball team, which won the state championship that year. The school still maintains the T, the third oldest hillside emblem in Nevada.
T	Tooele High School	Tooele, UT	Built in the early 1900s; still cared for and lighted as part of the school's homecoming activities.
T	Trona High School	Trona, CA	Every year since the T was built in 1942, the senior class has whitewashed it, and following that the freshmen have lighted it with thirty-minute railroad flares to begin homecoming weekend.
T	Tropic	Tropic, UT	Featured on page 153.
T	Tucumcari High School	Tucumcari, NM	The senior class takes a day off from school each year to paint the T.
TB	Twin Bridges High School	Twin Bridges, MT	Featured on page 157.

U UINTAH
Uintah, Utah

The built-up U located on the northern edge of Weber Canyon near Uintah, Utah, boasts one of the most dramatic beginnings of any western hillside letter in the country. The story begins about 1919, when Marlow J. Christensen was the principal of Uintah School. Back then the school was small and consisted of four classes with combined grades. The principal taught the oldest class, the seventh and eighth graders. Some of the boys in the seventh and eighth grade class were in their late teens. They were big, husky boys who had become so unruly and threatening that the principal had permission to carry a gun for self-defense.

On the evening of March 22, 1922, the friction between Christensen and two of the young men, Lloyd and Orville Bybee, ended with the tragic shooting of Orville by Christensen. Almost immediately the small town became divided over Christensen's actions. Eventually Christensen was found not guilty, but that did not end the division in the community.

A new replacement for Christensen, Golden Albert Kilburn, was quickly hired. This was the tenth principal of the school in six years. Many in the community believed there was no hope of changing the older boys' hostility towards school, but Mr. Kilburn did not share that belief. Soon after Kilburn took over, the older boys were up to their old tricks. According to Sue Bybee's "The Mountainside U," one day after the boys had thrown spitballs, been rude

This landmark letter U represents unity for the community of Uintah, Utah.

—UINTAH CITY HISTORICAL FILES

and hostile, and threatened to harm Kilburn, he walked to the classroom door and locked it. Then Kilburn said to the boys, "All right, if it's a fight you want, fine. I'll take you on one at time, or all of you at once." Kilburn, a former Navy man and one of his ship's best boxers, was in great physical shape and meant what he said. Only one young man stepped forward to meet Kilburn's challenge, and Kilburn gave him a "good trouncing." Kilburn then asked that not one word be said about what had happened, and added that if he found out someone had talked about it he would settle it with him personally.

The following day Kilburn was back at school with boxing gloves and baseball and basketball equipment for the boys. Choosing the boy he had "trounced" to help demonstrate, Kilburn began teaching the boys how to box and protect themselves. Kilburn's plan to help the boys also included sports and scouting. He organized the young men in his class and other boys in the community into a Boy Scout troop. The townsfolk later recalled that Kilburn often said, "There are no bad boys, we just have to help them expend their tremendous energy in the right directions."

As part of their requirements, the scouts had to participate in a church service. The local Mormon bishop agreed to have the boys speak, and Sunday evening the church was filled with all the folks from Uintah. The division of the town was still evident, with supporters of former principal Christensen sitting on one side of the church and opponents on the other. The scouts gave talks on "Loving My Neighbor," "Doing a Good Turn," and "Being Trustworthy." As the boys spoke, the mood of the congregation began to soften, and by the end of the evening old friends and neighbors crossed the aisle of the church and began embracing one another.

Thanks to Kilburn's efforts, the community of Uintah began to change. Shortly afterwards, Kilburn suggested that a U be built on the side of the mountain and that the scouts lead the project. The U would represent "Uintah," their town; "United" they stand; "Utah," their state; and the "United States," their country. During the winter of 1922, Kilburn had the scouts stand in the shape of the U on the mountainside to see how the letter would look. Later Kilburn and Norman Anderson, a resident of Uintah, returned and placed stakes in the ground to mark the spot where they would build the letter in the spring.

Even though the building of the U was meant to be a Boy Scout project, it was quickly evident that the scouts would need the help of the community. According to Bybee in "The Mountainside U," on April 28, 1923 "men, women, and kids went up; nearly everyone in town that could climb the mountain gave a hand" in building and whitewashing the 50-by-100-foot U.

As the years passed, an annual tradition of whitewashing and lighting the U became one of the most important events of the community. U Day started off

In 1922 the Boy Scouts of Uintah, Utah, stood on the snow-covered hillside in the shape of their future U. —UINTAH CITY HISTORICAL FILES

with the younger folks ringing cowbells or pulling tin cans and old tubs behind their cars, and it was usually an all-day affair with games, luncheon, parades, band concerts, and even the crowning of the U Day King and Queen.

In 2000 the Utah Division of Wildlife Resources restricted activities on the trail to the U due to environmental and private property issues. The U could no longer be painted or lighted. This was disappointing to many, and a group of citizens began working with the Utah Division of Wildlife Resources to obtain the right to rebuild and maintain the historic landmark U, and they also worked with a private citizen to gain access to the U across private property.

On June 12, 2004, after four years of negotiations and compromises, the community of Uintah lighted the U for the first time using electric lights. (Previously they had used oil with rags for wicks.) A year later a construction crew and some community members rebuilt the U. As of this writing, the new U is in the process of becoming a state historical landmark. The many community activities and events that surround the U continue to unite the town of Uintah, Utah.

U UNIVERSITY OF UTAH
Salt Lake City, Utah

If Professor Joseph F. Merrill had been on time for his Physics II class on April 20, 1905, there may not ever have been a letter U overlooking Salt Lake City, Utah. It started when sophomores Carl Scott and Richard Hart and a few others were assigned to cut the grass near the track for Arbor Day. The University of Utah used to celebrate Arbor Day each year by giving students the day off from classes so they could plant trees and care for the campus grounds. In a moment of inspired creativity, Scott began cutting in the tall grass the numbers 07, the graduation year for sophomores, and the others joined in. Hart suggested that they fill in the numbers with lime so the grass wouldn't grow back. Scott agreed, but wanted to move the numbers higher on the hill where everyone might see them, so they decided to wait until the next day.

The following day, when Professor Merrill didn't show up for class, Scott waited the mandatory fifteen minutes and then rallied his classmates to join him in placing a forty-foot-long 07 in lime on the hillside above campus. His enthusiastic classmates not only cut their Physics II class but skipped school the entire day. When the freshmen saw the 07, they weren't about to be outdone by the sophomores and quickly altered it to an 08. The two classes continued to change the forty-foot-long hillside numbers back and forth between

When a group of University of Utah students skipped their physics class back in 1905, they started a chain of events resulting in the giant U overlooking Salt Lake City, Utah. —PHOTO BY SARAH CORNING

This vintage postcard shows the students of the University of Utah painting their hillside U around 1907. —AUTHOR'S COLLECTION

07 and 08, using powdered lime to form numbers and dirt to cover them, until someone suggested that the classes unite and make a "mighty U," which would be, the 1909 yearbook later recorded, "an emblem of loyalty to the whole school."

Within days the students replaced the numbers with a U made with lime, under the direction of Hart, Scott, and their classmates. By the following spring the snow and rain of the winter had washed away much of the letter. In 1906 the students were given a special "half-holiday" to create a much larger U with lime. About six hundred students participated; the male students and faculty did the labor, passing up the hill an estimated five thousand buckets of lime, and the females provided a hearty lunch.

In 1907, student body president Stayner Richards suggested building a more permanent concrete U, which they did. Using several borrowed army mules, students completed the hundred-square-foot U in two and a half days. This U stood the test of time until 1969, when it was renovated with permanent power and lights at a cost of ten thousand dollars. The project required the joint effort of students, alumni, and administration. Because this hillside letter was built on federal land, renovations and new lighting also required an act of Congress (Senate Bill 1366).

For the next thirty-seven years the U was whitewashed and lighted for all major sporting events and special university functions. In fact, after a big home game many Salt Lake City residents just look out their windows at the lighted U to find out if the Utah Utes have won. If the lights on the U are blinking, the Utes have won. If they are not, the fans know that the Utes "stand steady" even in their loss.

In the fall of 2006, following a very successful fundraising campaign that raised over $650,000, the U was stabilized at a cost of $400,000. This was the fifth time the U was renovated by the university. The extra funds raised from the "Renew the U" campaign were used for additional student scholarships. The new and improved U, which incorporated the materials of the previous U, is equipped with the newest in computer-operated fiber-optic lights and has a sturdy enough foundation to keep it from sliding down the mountainside, as it had done in the past. Most importantly, the U has the overwhelming support of both the University and the people of Salt Lake City. With its high-tech upgrades, the University of Utah's U is both the oldest and the newest of the approximately fifty-seven hillside letters in the state.

	NAME	LOCATION	NOTE
U	Uintah	Uintah, UT	Featured on page160.
U	Ukiah	Ukiah, CA	A community letter made of large iron plates that the residents paint white.
U	University of New Mexico	Albuquerque, NM	The rock U was built on the foothills east of town sometime during the 1930s, and it was whitewashed by the freshman engineering students as part of their initiation until the 1960s. With the passage of time the old U has disappeared, but a group of alumni who call themselves Friends of the U get together to swap stories and memories of the days when the U adorned the hills of Albuquerque.
U	University of Utah	Salt Lake City, UT	Featured on page164.

V VALLEY HIGH SCHOOL
Orderville, Utah

In southern Utah, U.S. 89 travels through Long Valley, a beautiful area of red and white sandstone cliffs dotted with green meadows and meandering streams, where remnants of houses, barns, and other buildings dating back to the time of the original Utah pioneers can still be seen. Six miles north of the junction of U.S. 89 and Route 5 is Orderville, a small town of about six hundred residents. Orderville's name originated from the Mormon settlers' practice of owning things in common, called the "united order."

The site of the present Valley High School was the original school site during the time of the united order—from 1875 to the 1890s. The high school was built to serve the educational needs of the children who lived in several of the small communities in Long Valley. Behind the building is a long row of cream-colored sandstone cliffs, with one prominent rock visible in front of and just to the north of the cliff. The early settlers named this large boulder Chimney Rock, probably after the Chimney Rock in western Nebraska, which many of them had seen when they crossed the American continent as part of Brigham Young's emigration from Illinois to Utah in the 1840s. The original Chimney Rock had been an important landmark for these pioneers, and many had carved into the rock their names and the dates they passed by.

The Valley High School students, many of whom were descendants of those pioneers, chose Orderville's Chimney Rock as the location for their new

The V for Valley High School in Orderville, Utah, is painted on Chimney Rock.
—PHOTO BY JIM CORNING

Directly south of Valley High School's V is a cliff displaying the painted numbers of graduating class years as far back as the 1940s. —PHOTO BY JIM CORNING

school's hillside letter. Sometime in the 1930s the letter V was painted on the rock in the school colors, orange and black, with white added for accent. Like the pioneer companies of old who left behind their name and the date they passed by Nebraska's Chimney Rock, the senior classes of Valley High School leave behind the year they graduate on the cliff next to the Chimney Rock V. The earliest graduating year visible on the cliff is 1942. This tradition, well over half a century old, continues on today during the last week of school, when the seniors pick a spot on the cliff where they paint their class year. This is also the time when the old V gets its paint touched up, if necessary.

V VAN HORN HIGH SCHOOL
Van Horn, Texas

The rock V west of Van Horn, Texas, is on Turtleback Mountain, easily visible from Interstate 10. Turtleback Mountain is on Red Rock Ranch, a unique area of the Chihuahuan Desert that includes ancient petroglyphs and the largest Precambrian rock formations in North America. The town of Van Horn has a Wild West history. Local folklore says an early rancher named A. S. Goynes said of the climate, "The town is so healthy we'll have to shoot a man to start a cemetery." His statement hung in the lobby of the local hotel until Goynes was shot dead by his brother-in-law in a fight over a nearby watering hole. He became the first man buried in the Van Horn cemetery. Today this small community is a tourist stop for many travelers along Interstate 10 in far western Texas. Van Horn's V is one of about seventeen hillside letters found in the Texas panhandle.

The V was built sometime during the 1930s. No one is certain of what event prompted it, but all agree it was built as an emblem for Van Horn High School. In the beginning freshmen would paint the V once a year on Freshman Day. In the morning the freshmen would participate in activities at school, and in

The V on Turtleback Mountain, representing Van Horn High School, is a prominent landmark seen from Interstate 10. —PHOTO BY JIM CORNING

the afternoon the freshmen and seniors loaded up in the old school bus and headed to Turtleback Mountain, where both classes formed a bucket brigade up the hill to whitewash the V. In 1967, Red Rock Ranch changed hands, and the new owner, a retired military man, told the Van Horn High School students that unless he could ride along the road of his property without seeing any bottles or trash, they would not be allowed on his property to paint the V. The V remained unpainted for the next twenty-nine years.

In 1996, the fading white rock V was finally repainted, this time by the Van Horn Volunteer Fire Department, who now paint it every five years as part of an all-class reunion for the students of Van Horn High School and the Van Horn Jubilee.

	NAME	LOCATION	NOTE
V	Vale High School	Vale, OR	Made of pipes and maintained by the school.
V	Valley High School	Orderville, UT	Featured on page 168.
V	Valley Union High School	Elfrida, AZ	A whitewashed rock V outside of town.
V	Van Horn High School	Van Horn, TX	Featured on page 170.
V	Venice	Venice, UT	The whitewashed rock letter of this small town with no schools is kept looking good by church youth groups.
VC	Ventura College	Ventura, CA	The VC on the hills overlooking campus was the result of a campaign promise made by a candidate for student body president, Steven Warren, who promised to put Ventura College on the map, in part by building a hillside emblem. He was unable to fulfill his campaign promise while in office, but after his term he continued trying and finally succeeded. In April 1965 the engineering class surveyed the twenty-foot long letters. A local construction company donated equipment and the students provided the labor and materials to build the VC, which is still maintained today.
V	Victor High School	Victor, MT	A rock letter whitewashed by the freshmen while the seniors supervise.
V	Victorville	Victorville, CA	The V on Hospital Hill is considered a community letter, but the Victor Valley High School maintains and lights it yearly for their homecoming game.
V	Viewmont High School	Bountiful, UT	A concrete V maintained and painted by the students.
V	Virgin Valley High School	Mesquite, NV	A rock V maintained by the students.
V	Virginia City	Virginia City, NV	Built in 1926, the V is still maintained and is lighted every night; during the holidays the light color changes.

172

W WEBER STATE UNIVERSITY
Ogden, Utah

Weber State University's "Flaming W" began first as a large bonfire. Starting sometime in the late 1930s, the students of Weber College would hike every homecoming to Malan's Peak along the Wasatch Front. There the students would make a large fire and sit around the flames enthusiastically singing and chanting their school's fight songs and cheers. The homecoming bonfire was always large enough to be seen by the community, and it became known as the Flaming W.

From 1944 to 1946, the annual hike was discontinued because of the war. But as soon as the war was over and the young vets returned to campus, the homecoming hike to Malan's Peak was reinstated. Most years the students carried to the peak everything they needed to make a bonfire and roast a few hot dogs and marshmallows. One year, student and ex-military pilot Dick Farr flew over Malan's Peak and air-dropped wood, straw, and gasoline for the bonfire. The package burst and scattered on impact, and after that year the students went back to hauling the load for their homecoming bonfire on foot.

In the early 1950s, the school moved to its present campus, and in 1955 the students built a rock W on a grassy hill just east of campus. Two years later they cleared away dry grass from the area around the W in preparation for lighting their letter with red flares for homecoming. However, not enough ground was cleared, and when the students lit the flares that breezy night, some dry grass near the W caught fire. Flames quickly engulfed the hillside, burning grass and oak. Students, teachers, staff, and community members quickly ascended the hill and, using shovels and their own clothing, attempted to put out the flames. The Ogden City Fire Department and Forest Service firefighters arrived to help. By the time the fire was out, more than twenty-five acres had burned, and the college had to pay $1,500 in firefighting costs.

Geraldine Utzman, a student who was present during the blaze, saw the fire not as disaster but as an example of school spirit. In a letter to the editor of the student newspaper she said, "I am thankful to have had the eyewitness experience of observing the cumulative effects of the great traditions of Weber College's school spirit in motion. It is my opinion that the determination and courage personified in our [student] firefighters was just as brilliant as the fire itself."

For the next twenty-plus years, the school continued to light the W for homecoming, using electricity instead of flares. After the school became Weber State College in 1964, a rock S was added. Then sometime in the mid-1970s, due to erosion problems caused by hundreds of students climbing up and down the hillside to paint and light the WS, the school replaced the rock letters with a living hillside emblem. Students, staff, and community members donated sumac bushes, which were planted in the shape of the letter W. According to the plan, the sumac would turn bright red in the fall, creating a living Flaming W.

The living sumac emblem cost about $15,000, including planting hundreds of bushes, adding numerous bags of topsoil, building a pump on the hillside to provide the water, and laying a large drip irrigation system for the bushes. However, because of the poor soil and the many deer that enjoyed the taste of young sumac bushes, before long the living flaming W was gone.

Since 1980, Lynn Kraaima, a student at the school, and his childhood friend Rick Mitchell have rigged up lights in the shape of a slanted W for homecoming at the site of the old living emblem. In 1991 the school changed its name to Weber State University, and the W's shape changed to the Flaming W—a W shaped like a flame—that is presently used. For the past twenty-seven years, each day during homecoming week Kraaima and Mitchell have driven to the base of the W in a pickup truck with a generator in the back. They pull out their string of lights, wrap them around metal stakes outlining the shape of the Flaming W, and plug the lights into the generator. Kraaima and Mitchell stay at the truck from about dusk to eleven each night, reminiscing and visiting with families who bring their children by to see the Flaming W up close. If the children arrive early enough, the men let them light the W.

On the night of the homecoming game, Kraaima and Mitchell plug in the lights and turn on the radio to listen to the game. If the radio announcer reports that the Weber Wildcats have scored, the W blinks. When the Wildcats win their homecoming game, the blinker stays on until 1:00 a.m. to announce the victory. This method of lighting the school's letter isn't as sophisticated as the fiber optic systems used by some universities, but it is safer than fire, and as far as these two men are concerned their method is a lot more fun.

W WESTERN STATE COLLEGE OF COLORADO
Gunnison, Colorado

The inspiration for the W of Western State College of Colorado, located in Gunnison in west-central Colorado, resulted from John C. Johnson's visit in 1915 to the granddaddy of all hillside letters, the Big C at the University of California–Berkeley. While sitting on the Big C, Johnson became convinced that his school, Colorado State Normal School, needed a hillside N. Shortly after his return to Gunnison, Johnson inspired the student body to build an N on Smelter Hill just north of Western State's campus. This N was converted sometime after 1923 into a G for Gunnison County School, which at the time was the only high school in town. Today this old G is still a part of the Gunnison landscape.

In 1923 the governor of Colorado changed the name of the normal school to Western State College. A few days later, Johnson, who was now the dean at Western State College, once again promoted the building of a landmark letter for the school. His enthusiasm for building a W on the side of Tenderfoot Mountain south of the college easily convinced four students, Hugh Dowd, Burtis Adams, Nowell Hamm, and Herbert Axtell, to get involved. By the following day Johnson and his four student-helpers were on their way up Tenderfoot Mountain with a plan to build a three-hundred-square-foot W.

On the mountain the men found four dead evergreen trees, which they carried to where they thought the outer corners of the W should be located. They propped the trees up with heavy rocks and tied onto the trees white bedsheets

176

The W in Gunnison, Colorado, is the largest built-up hillside letter. —COURTESY OF WESTERN STATE COLLEGE OF COLORADO

that they had torn in half. Then the men headed back to campus to survey their outline. Viewing it from the football field, they realized their W was too small, so they returned to the mountain and moved the two lower trees a hundred feet lower down the hill. This decision to increase the size of the W resulted in the construction of the largest built-up letter in the nation.

A few days later the group was back on the hill, staking out the W in string, still using the four dead trees as the four outer corners of the W. On May 2, 1923, college president Samuel Quigley declared a school holiday to construct the W, and most of the Western State College students and faculty spent the day carrying thousands of flat rocks found on the hillside and placing them within the stringed outline of the W. As the years passed the emblem was whitewashed and cared for by the students of Western (see photos on pages 6 and 178).

In 1932, the built-up W was enhanced by adding serifs to the letter. Sometime during 1948, a rivalry developed between Western State College and

177

Students mix whitewash at the base of the W above Gunnison, Colorado (photo c. 1950).
—COURTESY OF WESTERN STATE COLLEGE OF COLORADO

Hundreds of Western State College students pass up buckets of whitewash to cover the W
(photo c. 1950). —COURTESY OF WESTERN STATE COLLEGE OF COLORADO

Brigham Young University, each claiming to have the largest college monogram. The staff of the Western's student newspaper, *Top of the World,* challenged Brigham Young University to "prove it." Western called in professor of mathematics Harvey C. McKenzie, who was supplied with pictures and measurements of both emblems. The W measured 320 feet wide and 420 feet long; the Y was 130 feet wide (at the top) and 380 feet long. After careful calculations and double-checking his slide rule, McKenzie found that Western State's W contained 25,560 square feet of rock and the Y of Brigham Young University contained 23,360 square feet (a number later confirmed by BYU). Western State College has a bigger letter than its much larger rival.

Grant Venn, a president of Western State College from 1960 to 1961, wrote that the school's W "symbolizes the kind of men and women, both students and faculty, who had the inspiration, the courage and the stick-to-itiveness to build and maintain the world's largest college symbol at one of the smallest colleges in the world. It means that the "W" . . . should help rekindle, in each of us, the desire to do the best job possible."

W WILLCOX
Willcox, Arizona

In the Circle I Hills near Interstate 10 in southeastern Arizona, the letter W stands for Willcox, Arizona, named for Orlando B. Willcox, the army general who arrived on the first train that rolled into town. This historic railroad community became known as the "cattle capital of the world" because it shipped more cattle by rail than any other town. Today, Willcox ships out thousands of cases of fruits and vegetables.

Seventeen-year-old Mike Bakarich designed the W for a Future Farmers of America project, and Willcox High School students built it in 1968 on Circle I Hills just north of town, overlooking some of Willcox's finest fields

The W that overlooks Willcox, Arizona, was built as a Future Farmers of America project in 1968. —PHOTO BY JIM CORNING

The W on Circle I Hills, which marks the location of Willcox, can be seen for miles around. —PHOTO BY JIM CORNING

and orchards. Circle I Hills, referred to by the students as W Mountain, is also home to some ancient Indian ruins and petroglyphs.

The freshman class, under the direction of the high school student council, hikes up Circle I Hills to whitewash the rock W each January, when it is usually cold enough that the rattlesnakes stay underground in hibernation. Today the W built and maintained by the Willcox High School students is considered both a school and a community letter.

	NAME	LOCATION	NOTE
W	University of Wyoming	Laramie, WY	The W was built in October 1913 by the freshman class on a small slope just north of campus. Maintenance of the letter ended about twenty years ago, but nearby homes are referred to as the W Hill neighborhood, and a street in town is named "W" Hill Road.
W	Wadsworth	Wadsworth, NV	Faded and no longer maintained.
WM	Wagon Mound	Wagon Mound, NM	These community letters were built one above the other, not side by side; they can be seen from Interstate 25.
W	Wahtonka High School	The Dalles, OR	A painted letter maintained by the students.
W	Weber State University	Ogden, UT	Featured on page 173.
W	Weed High School	Weed, CA	The student groups from the high school first gather donations of paint, then they take a field trip day to paint the W.
W	Weiser	Weiser, ID	The students at Weiser High School used to care for the W, but since the land has changed hands the letter is no longer maintained but is still visible.
W	Wells High School	Wells, NV	This rock letter is freshened up yearly by the high school booster club.
W	Wendover High School	Wendover, UT	Painted every year by the seniors, who add their class year beside it.
WS	West Side High School	Dayton, ID	The seniors whitewash the rock W during homecoming week.

	NAME	LOCATION	NOTE
W	Western New Mexico University	Silver City, NM	Each fall students, staff, and faculty paint the old rock W in an event called "The Painting of the W." The group climbs up to the letter and paints it white with brooms. The school hires a DJ to play music while the group paints, and everyone has a great time. Afterward the painters return to campus and receive a new T-shirt, designed by a student, to replace the paint-splattered shirt they are wearing. Then the school hosts an all-you-can-eat barbeque to finish off the day.
W	Western State College of Colorado	Gunnison, CO	Featured on page 176. See also photo on page 6.
WP	White Pine County High School	Ely, NV	Students began building the WP in 1941 just west of town and completed it the following year. They used to light their painted letter with bonfires during homecoming, but this is no longer done.
W	Whittier College	Whittier, CA	The concrete W has been around since the late 1960s. It is maintained and painted by the William Penn Society, a fraternal organization.
W	Willcox	Willcox, AZ	Featured on page 179.
W	Willits	Willits, CA	The W overlooking Willits is lighted every night, using solar panels installed as an Eagle Scout project.
W	Windham	Windham, MT	Built for the old Windham High School, which no longer exists.
WR	Window Rock School	Fort Defiance, AZ	The students at the K–12 Window Rock School paint the WR blue and white, their school colors.
W	Winifred High School	Winifred, MT	The W was built about 1958; the seniors still whitewash it each spring.
W	Winnemucca	Winnemucca, NV	The W was built to honor the Winnemucca High School girls' victory in the championship basketball game of 1920. However, the school no longer exists, so community groups now keep the W looking good. In March it is painted dark green, thanks to a local St. Patrick fan.
W	Winnett High School	Winnett, MT	This letter was built during the early 1940s. The freshmen paint it as part of their initiation, with the seniors ensuring that they do a good job.
W	Woodlake	Woodlake, CA	No longer maintained but still visible.
W	Wranglers of Wickenburg High School	Wickenburg, AZ	This rock W represents the Wranglers, the high school mascot. It is maintained by the students.

PHOENIX

PHOENIX
Mesa, Arizona

Every letter of the alphabet except X appears alone on one or more hillsides. Xavier is not an uncommon name for a school, but no school by that name has a hillside letter. There are only two towns in the United States that start with an X (both named Xenia), but neither one has a hillside letter, or even much of a hillside. No counties or states begin with X. There is no stand-alone landmark letter X. However, the letter X does appear in two hillside words: DIXIE (see page 50) and PHOENIX.

The giant rock word PHOENIX is in Usery Mountain Regional Park, twenty-one miles east of Phoenix, on the south side of Usery Mountain. Popular destinations in the park include the Wind Cave Trail and the beautiful hanging garden of rock daisies at Wind Cave, where visitors find a refreshing refuge from the Sonoran Desert heat. Many visitors at the park are also intrigued by the huge rock word PHOENIX built on a hillside about four hundred feet above the Usery Mountain Shooting Range.

The word PHOENIX forms the shaft of the arrow that points west towards Phoenix. The letters are 100 feet long and the entire word, including the arrow's pointer, is about 1,250 feet wide. The massive letters can be seen from the air at an altitude of 55,000 feet, and on land they are visible over thirty-five miles away. The best view along Route 60 is near the Ellsworth exit.

183

The X in the word PHOENIX, 100 feet tall, is one of two hillside Xs in the West. This giant arrow pointing toward Phoenix was constructed around fifty years ago by a group of Boy Scouts. —PHOTO BY SARAH CORNING

This hillside landmark was built by the Boy Scouts of America. The young scouts of Air Explorer Squadron No. 13, all between the ages of thirteen and seventeen, were some of the most determined letter builders in the country. Air Explorer Squadron No. 13, later known as Post 13, had been formed in 1949 under the leadership of Charles E. Merritt, and they met in a little Methodist Church in south Phoenix. Sometime in 1950, Merritt proposed that they build an air marker on the Superstition Mountains. That was quickly denied by government officials who thought it would disturb the natural wilderness, so Merritt and the boys turned their attention to the Usery Mountains and began building what has been called the world's largest air marker.

This was no easy scout project. The scouts worked at the site almost every weekend. They carried thousands of pounds of material up the mountain, including cement, lime, and three hundred pounds of dynamite. The U.S. Air

Force provided transportation to the Usery Mountain location from Williams Air Force Base. The boys dug, blasted, and hauled by hand hundreds of thousands of rocks to create the seven-lettered sign, which is as long as the Empire State Building is tall. When the rock letters were in place, Merritt and the boys mixed up a whopping 550 gallons of paint using Merritt's own recipe, which included white cement, lime, salt, and milk.

It took the scouts five and a half years to complete the project. When the huge air marker was finally finished, the squadron celebrated with a dedication ceremony on May 13, 1956, which included the crowning of an Air Marker Queen and two attendants. As a tribute to their efforts, Merritt's father, Edwin J. Merritt, built at the base of the marker a rock monument, which is still standing. On August 13, 1956, one Associated Newspapers article heralded the completion of this scout project: "A group of Boy Scouts in Phoenix, Ariz., have done a gigantic service to the nation and to mankind!"

Through the years, a couple of hillside letters have become official FAA visual landmarks: Cal Poly's P and the U in Uintah, Utah. However, the PHOENIX on Usery Mountain, now maintained by the Maricopa County Parks and Recreation Department, is probably the only hometown landmark originally built as an air marker for pilots.

	NAME	LOCATION	NOTE
X in DIXIE	Dixie High School	St. George, UT	Featured on page 50.
X in PHOENIX	Phoenix	Mesa, AZ	Featured on page 183.

Y BRIGHAM YOUNG UNIVERSITY
Provo, Utah

Ask a student at Brigham Young University what school they attend, and more than likely they will reply, "the Y." This hillside letter along the Wasatch Front east of the campus began with some controversy, but today it is considered an honored landmark.

P. C. Peterson, the editor of the student newspaper at Brigham Young University in Provo, Utah, had attended summer school at the University of California in Berkeley in 1905. After being very impressed with Berkeley's new hillside letter C, he proposed that the students at Brigham Young University build a hillside BYU for their school. His editorial of April 27, 1906, started a chain of events resulting in a hillside letter by June 1 of that year.

The school appointed a committee to consider building the letters; however, the committee must have moved too slowly, because the juniors surprised everyone by using lime to put their class year, 1907, on the mountainside. This led some seniors to retaliate by shaving the heads of a number of the junior boys, and even cutting the waist-length hair of a few junior girls. The juniors in turn justified their actions in a school newspaper article entitled "It Was Mean—But!" In it they explained that the student body wanted a hillside emblem immediately, and that the class of 1907 was just trying to arouse the necessary enthusiasm for it. To prevent further clashes, the university president, George H. Brimhall, called in engineering professor Ernest D. Partridge and asked him to design and supervise the construction of the school's three-lettered emblem.

The professor and three of his students, Elmer Jacob, Clarence Jacob, and Harvey Fletcher, climbed the mountain and secured a transit (a surveying instrument) at the proposed foot of the center letter. After they leveled the instrument, a telescope was set on a flagpole on campus. They read the inclination angle and began their calculations. The group had planned to stake out

The Y that stands for Brigham Young University in Provo, Utah, was the third hillside letter built in the country. It has been a favorite spot for marriage proposals. —PHOTO BY JIM CORNING

the letters on 280 acres of land the university had recently purchased for the project. However, they unknowingly staked out their school emblem on adjoining property belonging to the U.S. Forest Service. The next day a group of excited student body officers climbed up the steep hillside to view the newly staked-out letters before the rest of the young men arrived from campus to build the emblem. When the officers saw the letters up close, they initially refused to go to work on them because they thought they were disproportionate. Student body president Elmer Jacob persuaded his fellow officers that the design was correct when viewed from the perspective of campus.

When the other students arrived, the group started with the center letter, the Y. The work was backbreaking and took much longer than expected. Most of the young men had not eaten breakfast and thought the work of covering three giant letters in lime would be finished before noon. But passing the heavy bags of sand, rocks, and lime up the hill had been much more difficult than anyone had planned. Some of the young men fainted from exhaustion. By four that afternoon, only the Y was covered in a thin coat of lime. The worn-out young men gave up on the idea of covering the other two letters and returned to campus. However, when they looked back up and saw "a beautiful white 'Y' on the mountainside in just the right proportion," Fletcher later reported, they decided that the letter Y was enough.

The giant hillside Y covered in lime needed constant repair. The following year, 1907, the students added a layer of rock to the letter, and in 1908 a three-foot rim was constructed around the Y with twenty thousand pounds of sand and cement. In 1911 students added serifs to the letter. In 1913 a thousand pounds of concrete was poured on the lower part of the Y to stabilize it against erosion.

During those early years, male students were required to help with the care of the letter annually on Y Day. Those who did not risked having their head shaved as a warning to anyone who might consider not participating in the

Y's maintenance. Despite the presence of young men with no hair on campus today, this practice was discontinued years ago.

Each year since 1913 more concrete has been added to the letter to stabilize it, eventually turning the original lime Y into a giant built-up letter made of concrete and stone. Because the letter had mistakenly been built on Forest Service land, the annual student-led whitewashing of the letter ended in 1982 when the Forest Service prohibited it due to environmental concerns about erosion caused by foot traffic. Since then the school has hired a helicopter to haul paint, sprayers, and water. Brigham Young University has never added a B or U to their beloved Y, now over a century old.

	NAME	LOCATION	NOTE
Y	Brigham Young University	Provo, UT	Featured on page 186.
Y	Yarnell	Yarnell, AZ	The rock Y in this small community is maintained by the local chamber of commerce.
Y	Yerington	Yerington, NV	A whitewashed rock community letter; painted by Yerington High School students and alumni.
Y	Yreka	Yreka, CA	Because this letter is formed with loose white boards, chances of seeing the Y are not very good. The townsfolk and students from Yreka High School often transform the Y into other emblems, such as the graduating year of a particular class, the initials of a person in the community they want to honor, or even an M for Miners, the school mascot.
Y	Yucaipa High School	Yucaipa, CA	The Y is cared for by a group of students called the Block Y Club, who keep it looking good and light it for the homecoming football game.

Z ZAP
Zap, North Dakota

The only hillside Z is cradled in the beautiful rolling hills of North Dakota. It can be seen north of Route 200 overlooking the close-knit community of Zap. Zap is a small town by area and population, with just a little over two hundred people and city limits covering only one square mile. To locals Zap is affectionately known as "the little town with a big heart." Zap may be more widely known for a riot that occurred there in 1969, when between two and three thousand college students came to Zap for "a grand festival of life and love." This event, known as the "Zip to Zap," began as a joke in a college newspaper but word spread and the crowds poured in. The unplanned party quickly got out of hand. During the weekend escapade, the students drank everything in the two local bars, burned a tumbled-down building, and in general raised havoc. This was too much even for the big heart of Zap. The town called in the National Guard and had the students zipped out of town.

Nine years earlier, in 1960, Custer Solem became the new superintendent of schools in Zap. Solem thought that hillside letters were a fine addition to any community's landscape, and he thought Zap would be a wonderful place for a Z. It wasn't long before his two sons Robert and Ray, a few other local boys, and a couple of farmers with trucks were on a hillside south of town building the Z. Solem, a former Boy Scout, positioned himself about a mile away with flags to signal the workers how to place the rocks on the hill. His flag system was not successful, however, so Solem returned to the hill and helped the boys

The Z in Zap, North Dakota, is the only hillside Z in the nation. The orange and black stripes represent the old school colors before the district dissolved years ago.
—PHOTO BY ROBERT SOLEM

The Z in Zap, North Dakota, shortly after it was built in 1960.
—COURTESY OF ROBERT SOLEM

move the hundreds of rocks needed to form the Z. By the end of the day the tired group had completed the job. Soon afterwards, the freshmen at Zap High School whitewashed the letter as part of their initiation.

The population of Zap has decreased since the 1960s, and the town no longer has a school. Now the residents of Zap proudly care for the only hillside Z in the country.

	NAME	LOCATION	NOTE
Z	Zap	Zap, ND	Featured on page 190.

For over a century, giant letters have been constructed with youthful energy upon hillsides, buttes, cliffs, and mountains. Most prevalent in the western United States, these hillside letters have changed not only the American landscape but also our culture. Many of these letters carry rich traditions that have influenced entire communities or schools for decades. More than just rock, concrete, or paint, these emblems are places where students and community members come to associate, renew old ties, follow traditions, and engage in rites of passage.

Newcomers to the West or well-meaning officials who see hillside letters as eyesores or liabilities may be surprised at locals' emotional outcry at the suggestion that a letter be removed. But personal aesthetics and environmental impacts aside, any value judgment would be incomplete without considering the rich history and cultural traditions associated with many of these letters. Hillside letters are not just signposts; they symbolize the heart and soul of the community or school they represent.

Invitation to the Reader

If you know of a hillside letter that isn't listed in this book, or if you have a story or photo of a letter that you would like to share, the author would love to hear from you. You can contact Evelyn Corning at the Hillside Letters Web site: www.hillsideletters.com.

BIBLIOGRAPHY

"155 Gallons Cover the Y." *Daily Universe*, June, 19, 1990.

Adair, Ella. "Tropic and Bryce Valley High Schools Historical Information." Bryce Valley High School. www.geocities.com/brycevalley/History/History.html.

"'A' Day." *Swastika*. New Mexico Agricultural College yearbook, 1925.

Arizona State University. "'A' Mountain." www.asu.edu/tour/main/amtn.html.

Ball, Phyllis. *Photographic History of the University of Arizona 1885–1985*. Tucson: Isbell Printing Company, 1986.

"The Big C and a New Tradition." *The Blue and Gold*, University of California–Berkeley yearbook, 1906.

Bryce Canyon National Park. "History and Culture." www.nps.gov/brca/history culture/index.htm.

Butterworth, Edwin, Jr. *Brigham Young University: 1,000 Views of 100 Years*. Provo: Brigham Young University Press, 1975.

Bybee, Sue. "The Mountainside U." Uintah City Historical Files, 2005.

Cahoon, Cliff. "History of the Lighting of the A on the Mountain." Merrill Library Archives, Utah State University.

Cal Poly. "Legacy of the Poly P." www.calpoly.edu/~rtclub/rthist.html.

Campbell, Kara and Katrina Brainard. "What Is That 'I'?" *Utah Statesman*, February 26, 2003.

Church of Jesus Christ of Latter-day Saints. "Chimney Rock: Life on the Mormon Trail." www.lds.org/gospellibrary/pioneer/20_Chimney_Rock.html.

Colorado School of Mines. "History of the 'M.'" www.mines.edu/all_about/history/historyofm.html.

Crowder, David L. *The Spirit of Ricks: A History of Ricks College*. Rexburg: Ricks College Publisher, 1997.

Cundiff, Rosemary, comp. "Agency History." Utah History Research Center, May 2003. historyresearch.utah.gov/agencyhistories/746.html.

"Dedication of the Monument to Colonel Charles DeBrille Poston." *Arizona Blade-Tribune*, May 9, 1925.

Devlin, Sherry. "One 'L' of a Design." *Missoulian*, October 31, 1998.

Duarte Historical Society. "Duarte, the Man." Pamphlet, Duarte, Calif.

"Elko High School Teacher Dies in Ruby Mountains from Exposure in Storm." *Elko Free Press*, October 2, 1916.

Finacom, Steven. "Building the Big C." *California Monthly*, November 2000.

"First Person: Y Mountain Memories." *BYU Magazine*, Summer 2006.

Freese, Natalie M. "Charter Hill and the Big C." Unpublished history.

"Governor Lights 'M.'" *Montana School of Mines Amplifier*, May 16, 1962.

Graham, Andrea. "If It's 'T' It Must Be Tonopah." *Nevada Magazine*, September/October 1978.

Hall, Barbara Ann, and Odette Marie Pietzsch, comps. *Mt. San Antonio College—The First Fifty Years*. Walnut, Calif.: Mount San Antonio Research Office, 1996.

Hansen, James E., II. *Democracy's College in the Centennial State—A History of Colorado State University*. Fort Collins: Colorado State University, 1977.

Hickson, Howard. "The Big 'E.'" Howard Hickson's Histories. www.outbacknevada.us/hickson/bige.html.

"'H' on Lookout Mountain." *Black Hills Pioneer*.

Idaho State University. "History of Idaho State University." www.isu.edu/departments/urelate/longhistory.html.

Jennings, Keith. "'A' on Tempe Butte Part of ASU's Local History." Arizona State University. www.asu.edu/news.

Maresh, Michael. "Group Works to Restore Bisbee B to Original Glory." *Sierra Vista Herald*, January 29, 2006.

Marshall, Con. *Continuing to Thrive after Seventy-Five Years—Story of Chadron State College 1911–1986*. Fremont, South Dakota: Pine Hill Press, 1986.

McGlynn, Terrence. *Montana Tech 1893-1984*. Butte: Montana Tech Foundation, 1984.

"M-Day History." Merrill G. Burlingame Special Collections. Bozeman: Montana State University.

Merritt, Charles E. Letter to Air Explorer Squadron No. 13, August 11, 1979.

"M to Be Lighted." *Montana School of Mines Amplifier*, May 1, 1962.

New Mexico Agricultural College. "Aggies Construct Large 'A' on Tortugas." *Round Up*, April 1920.

New Mexico Agricultural College. "Large 'A' to Be Built on Tortugus." *Round Up*, March 30, 1920.

Olson, Diane. *Idaho State University—A Centennial Chronicle*. Pocatello: Idaho State University, 2000.

Olson, Eric. "Crews Battle to Stop Blazes." *Lincoln Daily Journal*, July 2006.

Parsons, James J. "Hillside Letters in the Western Landscape." *Landscape*, November 1, 1988.

"Remembrances of the First D-Day." *Dixie Day Spectrum/Advertiser*, April 20, 1983.

Rhoads, Sam, ed. "A History of the World's Largest College Emblem." Unpublished history, May 6, 1961.

Rocha, Guy. "Hillside Letter: In Plain Site but Not Intended for Planes." *Sierra Sage*, June 2004.

Seal, Franklin. "Return of the G: Alumni Restore Block Letter to Moab Cliff." *Times-Independent*, August 10, 2000.

Skousen, W. Cleon, and Ernest L. Wilkinson. *Brigham Young University: A School of Destiny*. Provo: Brigham Young University Press, 1976.

Sorgenfrei, Robert. "A 'Blast' from the Past: The Football Season of 1919." *Mines Magazine*, November/December 1999. www.alumnifriends.mines.edu/fun_stuff/football_1919/default.htm.

"Story of the U." *Utonian*, University of Utah yearbook, 1909.

Stymiest, Ruth Anne. *Centennial—An Illustrated History 1885-1985*. Rapid City: Media Center of South Dakota School of Mines and Technology, 1985.

"Tintic High School Student Body Celebrate First Anniversary of 'T' Day." *Eureka Reporter*, May 9,1913.

"Traditions: Painting and Lighting the 'M.'" *1993 Missoula Visitors Guide*, University of Montana Centennial Issue. Missoula: Inter-Mountain Marketing, 1993.

University of Arizona. "The McKale Era—Building an Athletic Tradition." www.arizona .edu/tours/history/history8.php.

University of Nevada–Reno. "Huge Block N Grows Rapidly." *Sagebrush*, April 22, 1913.

University of Nevada–Reno. "Huge Block N on Peavine." *Sagebrush*, April 15, 1913.

Wakida, Penny, and Leslie Hiraga, eds. "Lahainaluna High School 175th Anniversary Commemorative Booklet." Wailuku, Hawaii: Ace Publishing, 2006.

Western Montana College Centennial Book: 1893-1993 100 Year History of Excellence. Logan, Utah: Herff-Jones Company, 1993.

White, W. P. "The Origin of the Garibaldi 'G.'" Unpublished history available through Friends of the G, Garibaldi, Oregon.

Wilson, Dan. "The Class of 1929 Built the 'O' to Last." *Oroville Mercury Register*, March 30. 1989.

INDEX BY STATE

This index lists the letter sites—the towns and schools that hillside letters represent—and is organized by state.

- Entries contain both town and school if a letter represents both.
- PARENTHESES: location of school
- BOLD: page numbers of featured letters
- ITALIC: page numbers of photographs

ABOUT THE AUTHOR

Evelyn Lyman Corning grew up in the quiet southern Utah town of Escalante, where she developed an early fascination for the large whitewashed E on a nearby hillside. She graduated from Southern Utah State College with a degree in elementary education, worked for the National Parks Service, and taught school. Corning has authored a number of articles for newspapers and magazines; *Hillside Letters A to Z: A Guide to Hometown Landmarks* is her first book. She and her husband, Jim, have five children and live in Tucson, Arizona, the home of a hillside A.